Sarah Sands is a former newspaper editor and editor of the Radio 4 Today programme. Her previous book was *The Interior Silence, 10 monastic lessons*.

For Kim Fletcher.

Sarah Sands

In Search of the Queen of Sheba

Austin Macauley Publishers

LONDON * CAMBRIDGE * NEW YORK * SHARJAH

A CIP catalogue record for this title is available from the British Library.

ISBN9781398460669 (Paperback)
ISBN 9781398460676 (Hardback)
ISBN9781398460683 (ePub e-book)

www.austinmacauley.com

First Published 2022
Austin Macauley Publishers Ltd®
1 Canada Square
Canary Wharf
London
E14 5AA

I would like to thank the academics, archaeologists and fellow travellers who shared my enthusiasm for the Queen of Sheba and were willing to pass on their wisdom so that I could search for hers.

Table of Contents

Preface
Ethiopia, London, Norfolk, March

I am standing on a quay in Salalah, a modern, industrial port in the south-east corner of the Sultanate of Oman. We're surrounded by elaborate security fences, for while Oman is a peaceful country, this is a dangerous region. To the west is Yemen, currently riven by war. To the north sit Saudi Arabia, Egypt and—if you go a little further—Israel. The Arabian Sea in these southern reaches is a thoroughfare for terrorists, pirates and drug runners.

There's a land route from here to Israel and the ancient city of Jerusalem, crossing 1,500 miles of desert. Or it's possible to get most of the way there by sea, which is what has brought me here. I've just arrived to find the elegant, pale grey, deadly shape of HMS Dragon, a British Royal Navy Type 45 Destroyer. Dragon is heading for the Red Sea, through the Suez Canal and into the Mediterranean and I am hitching a lift on her. Her: ships take the female pronoun; feminine might.

I had to come because, perhaps 3,000 years before me, another woman stood on this shoreline to board a ship. I'd seen her in a painting in the National Gallery in London, by the French artist Claude Lorrain. In 1648, he imagined a similarly bustling port, a scene of ships, laden with exotic cargoes, sailing towards measureless horizons. His picture is a representation of the moment a storied, iconic ruler left her fabled lands in Arabia to journey to mighty Jerusalem, in response to an invitation from another great monarch, King Solomon, the son of King David. His picture is the Embarkation of the Queen of Sheba.

That mission by a travelling monarch was to create an astonishing, lasting celebrity for the Queen of Sheba, securing her a place in the Bible and in the Koran and capturing the imagination of the three great Abrahamic faiths. She's a sliver of an Old Testament story that has excited celebrated artists, writers and musicians; a figure immortalised in the statuary and stained glass windows of great cathedrals, a character who finds a new life today in—for heaven's sake—a music video by Beyonce.

In the Bible, she seeks wisdom and comes to test King Solomon with hard questions, in return for 'all she desired'. Many believe that some of the most erotic verses ever written—the *Song of Songs*—celebrate their union. The account in the Koran is different: she submits to King Suleiman, a pagan queen converting to Suleiman's God, who is Allah. Was her embassy to the north an early international trade mission, bringing valuable frankincense and gold to burnish the reputation of King Solomon and the city-state of Jerusalem? Or did she travel as a temptress, lover and destroyer?

Hers remains a name of colossal fame, on ships, hotels, restaurants, stamps and beauty products. She is an image in stained glass at Canterbury Cathedral, England, a cartoon on a vacuum pack of coffee on an Ethiopian market stall. My hotel in Salalah welcomed me with a 'Sheba cocktail'; at another, just along the waterfront from this harbour, I am encouraged to dine in Sheba's Steakhouse. Many of us heard about the queen without any idea who she was, a saying from our childhoods, used against any woman who courted luxury or threatened to get above her station: "Who does she think she is, the Queen of Sheba?"

Across three millennia, her story resonates a queen who, alone in the Old Testament, held territorial power in her own right; a woman of nobility and diplomacy who went to discover the truth about power. Still, she retains that force and mystery. She is ancient and modern, black, female, potent. Her guises, from virtuous woman to femme fatale, stateswoman to the witch, reflect the conflicting emotions a male-dominated world has towards women, quick to place them on a pedestal or to denigrate and condemn.

In the current social and political turmoil about relationships between men and women and global power and trade, the nature of the queen of Sheba becomes an intriguing question. She had beauty and she sought wisdom. Her wisdom touches faith, philosophy and reason. But we are attributing all this to a woman who walked the lands of the Middle East as much as a millennium before Jesus Christ. Did she exist, or have we invented her?

Chapter 1
Ethiopia, March

My single-minded interest in the Queen of Sheba began a year earlier, on a hot and dusty day in Axum, northern Ethiopia.

It is a small town but an ancient kingdom. Axum claims to have a unique treasure, which makes it a shining city on a hill. Axum is where the Ark of the Covenant is said to reside; The Ark holds the tablets of Moses, brought down from the mountain of Sinai. Axum then is where pilgrims seek the literal word of God.

I rest against a wall. I have come with a reporter and a producer from the BBC to mark Easter in this devout place. It is pleasant here in this tree-shaded square of St Mary of Zion. I come from a restless city where everybody is in the move. Here, people sit and watch, steeped in the past.

Priests and monks, in the Coptic tradition, lead a procession around the raised church—some in richly coloured robes, carrying silk umbrellas, others in ethereal white. We are witnessing Easter when Christians join in the despair and joy at the crucifixion and resurrection of Christ.

But the ceremony, the symbols and the people speak of an older, Old Testament tradition influenced by the customs of southern Arabia.

The city of Axum feels ancient and mystical. While Ethiopia—previously Abyssinia—is a modern democracy, recovering from a recent history of conflict and famine, it is also a land of legend and treasure, a fabled place sought over centuries by explorers, missionaries, historians and archaeologists.

It is the middle of the day and I retreat into the shade, where the women and the maimed form a second circle congregation. Above us in the cloudless sky, kites circle. I peer over the wall at the ruins of a temple and a monastery beyond. To one side, is the plain chapel, from which a robed priest slips through an entrance.

What he guards is so precious and secret that nobody but he will ever see it.

But how are we supposed to believe in it if we cannot see it? The Ethiopian clergy shrug: believe it or don't believe it, they have it. I screw up my eyes against the sun to take in the deceptively utilitarian looking chapel. Could I at least approach it through the path that leads to the monastery?

Nobody but the priest is permitted to enter the chapel and no women are allowed on the monastery path. The reason for this, says my sheepish guide, is the ruins of a temple in front of the monastery and the chapel of the Ark.

A hot-tempered pagan queen, named Gudit, destroyed the temple along with the rest of the region in the tenth century. Her name meant fire, and she breathed revenge. I am interested that Ethiopia produced such powerful women during this time, even if flamboyantly monstrous ones.

My male colleagues disappear down the path while I stay behind. I find a bench under a flowering mimosa tree and take out a bottle of water from my bag. There are only women around me, and we exchange discreet glances and smiles.

They are allowed into St Mary Zion church but they are happy merely to be close to it. The square is a place to gather. It is as if the shadow of Gudit—who sounds rather like Queen of the Night from Mozart's opera, *The Magic Flute*—has left behind a female chorus to atone for her. The myths of the past eclipse the present.

I follow a flash of red, the African firefinch, hopping from branch to branch. He takes me beyond the precincts past the traders.

It is haphazard here, away from the ceremonial orderliness of the church square. Young boys approach me with souvenir icons, a plastic replica of the Ark of the Covenant, some tiny, soil-covered ancient coins they have dug up. I shake my head regretfully at the coins. That is their heritage.

I keep walking and come to a stone entrance and beyond it a simple seminary. In the doorway of a cell-like room, I find a slender, large-eyed nun, looking out at the comings and goings of the world. Two younger women sit like handmaidens on either side, reciting prayers in an incantatory murmur that discourages interruption.

In this setting of piety, the nun has a bright, knowing expression and regards the paraphernalia of broadcasting in my rucksack—microphone, digital recorder—wryly. She does not wish to be named or photographed but is happy to talk and has enough English to sustain a conversation.

I ask who or what inspires her, expecting an answer of orthodox piety, perhaps a Christian saint, or a local nun. Her answer brings me up short: "The Queen of Sheba. Because she had beauty, but she sought wisdom."

14

One of the novice nuns adds: "Because of her, the Ark of the Covenant came here."

The Queen of Sheba! I have not heard the name since childhood, as a rebuke to women who do not know their place. "Who does she think she is? The Queen of Sheba?" She was a woman of unreachable splendour.

It is a name redolent of luxury and exoticism and ambition. But I have no idea who she is or why her name should be mentioned here, in Axum. Yet, here is a nun introducing her as a figure of religious inspiration, a woman who knew something so important that she is worthy of study thousands of years later. She had beauty but sought wisdom sounds like the answer to a riddle. What was the wisdom she was searching for, and did she find it? And what did she have to do with the Ark of the Covenant?

I read the title of the Queen of Sheba blazoned across the sides of Ethiopian planes. She represents travel, after all. But where did she come from? Where was she going? Could I follow her or would it just be a wild goose chase?

I return to the hotel in Addis, on a road that is straining to be a business quarter once the Wi-Fi and potholes are fixed. The curtains are so thin they tear at the touch. The struggle to accommodate the uniform demands of the international traveller only throws into relief the unique richness of the heritage.

I look out of the window at the scaffolding and concrete of the half-built neighbouring office block.

On my small, reproduction bedside table is a copy of Gideon's Bible. I am pretty sure the Queen of Sheba was in the Old Testament, but am uncertain about where.

I start with Genesis and the story of Creation. Here is Eve, the first woman, the temptress, the origin of sin.

Later comes Abraham and his wife Sarah, who bore him no children and her Egyptian handmaid Hagar, who did bear Abraham a son, called Ishmael. In extreme old age, Sarah then conceived Isaac.

In Islam, Ishmael is a prophet and an ancestor of Muhammad. Isaac takes us to Moses, down to King David and his son Solomon, the story of the Jewish faith. The light outside fades and I turn on my rickety bedside lamp, knees up turning the fine pages, absorbing the storms of retribution and forgiveness of the Old Testament through dynastic lines.

Then I get to Kings 1, chapter 10. A new character, unconnected to all the fathers, appears. She is a Queen in her own right and she has arrived from an

15

unknown country to see Solomon. This is what we know, in thirteen verses of the Queen of Sheba:

1. And when the Queen of Sheba heard of the fame of Solomon concerning the name of the Lord, she came to prove him with hard questions.
2. And she came to Jerusalem with a very great train, with camels that bare spices and very much gold, and precious stones and when she came to Solomon she communed with him of all that was in her heart.
3. And Solomon told her all her questions there was not anything hidden from the king which he told her not.
4. And when the Queen of Sheba had seen all Solomon's wisdom and the house that he had built.
5. And the meat of his table and the sitting of his servants and the attendance of his ministers and their apparel and his cupbearers and his ascent by which he went up unto the house of the Lord; there was no more spirit in her.
6. And she said to the king, It was a true report that I heard in mine own land of thy acts and thy wisdom.
7. Howbeit I believed not the words and I came and my eyes had seen it and behold the half was not told me; thy kingdom and prosperity exceedeth the fame which I heard.
8. Happy are the men, happy are these thy servants, which stand continually before thee, and that hear thy wisdom.
9. Blessed be the Lord they God which delighted in thee, to set thee on the throne of Israel; because the Lord loved Israel forever; therefore made her thee king, to do judgement and justice.
10. And she gave the king a hundred and twenty talents of gold and spices very great store and precious stones; there came no more such abundance of spices as these which the Queen of Sheba gave to King Solomon.
11. And the navy also of Hiram that brought gold from Ophir, brought in from Ophir great plenty of almug trees and precious stones.
12. And the king made of the almug trees pillars for the house of the Lord and for the king's house, harps also and psalteries for singers; there came no such almug trees nor were seen unto this day.
13. And King Solomon gave unto the Queen of Sheba all her desire, whatsoever she asked, beside that which Solomon gave her of his royal bounty. So she turned and went to her own country, she and her servants.

Her entire story is in thirteen verses, yet it has spread far beyond these pages, echoed in the Koran, crossing borders and seas. It is a story, in other words, which is terribly hard to get into a linear order. I am not sure how to tell it let alone how to sell it. But what a woman she was! I owe it to her to try. I need to go back to the beginning. I see that the quest is going to be consuming. The Queen of Sheba bore witness and she asked questions.

She was a reporter, although she travelled with a large entourage and was hugely rich, unlike the reporters that I know. There was a quality to her questions that revealed essential truths.

My last job as an editor of a current affairs programme was to think up questions for politicians to answer. These are called accountability interviews. How much will this cost? Why do you say this when previously you said that? Apologise! Resign!

The Queen of Sheba asked hard questions in a different way. She was pursuing different ends. She was testing Solomon against his reputation. She was asking the question: Are we as we appear?

She was looking for deeper meanings and used different methods. As I look further into her hard questions, I see how elusive they are. She is talking in riddles. The deepest meaning does not fit into a news format. I must try different methods.

The first thing you are taught by local newspaper editors is to address four questions. Who, what, where, why? I realise I do not know the answer to any of these questions. I do not know who or what she was. I don't know where she came from and I do not know why she travelled. I am going to have to start at the beginning. I have no idea where it will end. This is not a quest like anything I have known before.

There is a destination—Jerusalem. There is a city of gold which is Ophir. Perhaps it has another name. I must try to work out geography and establish history. The why is central, and it may lead to the what. The Queen of Sheba is a figure of myth and of faith. The nun said that she obtained wisdom.

I wonder if I can find any traces of her in the red volcanic rock of the Ethiopian highlands, where the monolithic churches are hewn. Should I look for her in wall paintings, in the flight of the native black-winged lovebird, or in the delicate high cheek boned beauty of some of the young Ethiopian women?

The Queen of Sheba is a mystery. She was opulent. What was the source of her wealth, and where was her land? She and King Solomon understood each other, he kept nothing from her and he gave her all she desired.

Is this a deeply erotic metaphor or is it an allegory?

And what was the significance of the navy and its exploration of fabled places?

I know that the answers will not be easy to find. Ethiopia is the land of the occult. Its secrets are kept within its monasteries, formed from the very rocks. Look high up into the mountain boulders, and you may see the movement of a figure in white.

A priest, carrying goatskin pages of the gospel, it is a place of low, narrow, mud-brick doorways, and candlelight. Is this where I will unravel the myth of the Queen of Sheba?

I have started to collect maps of the region and lay them out. Here I am in the heights of Ethiopia. I am bordering Sudan to the west, Eritrea to the south, Djibouti and the Horn of Africa to the east. Across the Red Sea and the Gulf of Aden are Yemen and Oman. If you follow the Red Sea north you pass Egypt on one side, Saudi on the other. Beyond Saudi is Jordan, Palestine, Israel, Jerusalem.

This is where I must search for the Queen of Sheba, using the clues of the thirteen verses. As it turns out, this becomes my odyssey.

Back in London, in a bustling newsroom, the Queen of Sheba seems far away. There is a political crisis, there is conflict in Jerusalem over the moving of the Israeli embassy, there are military concerns over the role of Iran in the Gulf. But she speaks to me still across the ages. My professional career is a series of loose ends. Stories come and go. This is one that I want to see through to the end. It is not an assignment but an unfolding mystery.

My colleagues started to squint at the titles of Amazon books arriving on my desk. *Ethiopian Magic Scrolls*, *Holy City and the Grail*, and *The Worship of the Serpent, Enigmas and Riddles*.

"Everything OK?" asks my political editor.

I am also in flux in my personal life. My children have grown up and left home. I am freer to complete my own journey.

I walk with my husband along the Norfolk coast, near our home, the best way to clear my head. I love this stretch of sand; it is flat and empty and blasted by Siberian winds under the wide, low Norfolk skies. In the summer, the cavalry brings the horses here for holidays. They gallop through the spray then wade out until they are up to their girths. It is to be an image of perfect freedom.

I start to gabble to my husband about the Queen of Sheba and he indulges me. Others less so. When I start talking about her during a dinner with a famously impatient art collector, my husband kicks me under the table. The art dealer's face is clouding over. I try to interest him in Claude Lorrain, but his period is contemporary. He asks me if it is a bit like the Game of Thrones and I shake my head and start to quote Genesis, Exodus, Numbers, and most relevant, Kings and Chronicles. I have lost the audience. I apologise on the way home, but I am not really sorry. I have only discovered the narrative allure of the Bible.

The point of the Queen of Sheba is that she is a journey. She may be a chimera in the Bible but I can trace her footsteps.

I am off on an escapade. There is so much to do. I need to read, to plot, to navigate. I need to find a route, literal and metaphysical.

Even the news schedules of the day are leading me back to the Queen of Sheba.

The Red Sea has become more dangerous now than then. Jerusalem is as central and fought over now as then. Trade and power are intimately related. This journey into the past will return me to the present. It is one of the ancient world's greatest stories and I intend to crack it.

On the paving stones outside the BBC, offices are written in brass, resonant names, some countries, some cities, some past, some present. I always stop to look across at them, hopscotch of geography. Odessa, Peking, Constantinople, Rubicon, Crimea, Khartoum, Ypres, Jordan, Waterloo, Patagonia, Euphrates, Nile, Petra, Oman, Addis Ababa, San Sebastian, Aden, California, Damascus, Jerusalem. And I make a note: Addis Ababa, Oman, Aden, Jordan, Jerusalem. I need a map. I need a globe.

I walk briskly past crowded streets and squares to the British Museum. Through the Egyptian rooms, past the Assyrians, and the Babylonians, there are no rooms for a 3,000–year-old civilisation named Sheba. Even if she did not exist, it became necessary to invent her.

When the British Museum staged an exhibition of the Queen of Sheba twenty years ago, it included Yemeni stamps, a Japanese coffee drink called the Queen of Sheba and a poster of Gina Lollobrigida in a hot tub.

But they had one ancient artefact to make you gasp. It was a beautiful alabaster head of a woman known only as Myriam. The funerary bust had been found in Yemen, at Timna cemetery, near Marib, by the dashing American explorer Wendell Phillips, in the 1950s and is dated to the first millennium BC.

Myriam had dark, unseeing once lapis lazuli bejewelled eyes, perfectly drawn eyebrows, a straight nose, a half-smile, a long graceful neck. She gave nothing away and yet was irresistible. Her beauty was suggestive and secret. I buy a postcard of Myriam from the British Museum shop and put it on my desk on top of my books. I am starting to collect clues and mementos to build up the case for my Queen of Sheba. I am starting to scribble down words. They are all followed by question marks. And I remind myself not to scramble down too many rabbit holes.

I remember the painting in the National Gallery by Claude Lorrain. I think of the woman standing on a shoreline waiting to board a ship, which will take her into a path of light shimmering towards the horizon. She is sailing into the unknown. The Embarkation of the Queen of Sheba.

The title is my inspiration. It gives no detail of the journey itself; the embarkation is the important thing. Voyages are self-discoveries. I am determined now to go.

I think if I can follow her journey, I may be able to crack the riddle of the Queen of Sheba.

Chapter 2
Norfolk, Canterbury, Cologne, Cambridge, April My Pilgrimage

It is spring in Norfolk. The cherry trees cast their soft blossom into the breeze, the daffodils form a guard of honour along the front path, tilting yellow trumpets. But my thoughts are in the Middle East. The Queen of Sheba represents the other, the hidden, the elusive to me. She divides into multiple selves.

There are at least three versions of the Queen of Sheba. There is the Queen of Sheba in the Old Testament. She then becomes Queen Bilquis of Saba in Arab lore and she is Makeda in the old scripture of Ethiopia. I know where Ethiopia is, I know where Jerusalem is but Saba? Three identities, three claims to fame, three sets of believers. She speaks in riddles and to different audiences. The Queen of Sheba is cast and re-cast through time and place.

What is extraordinary about the Queen of Sheba is how she is realised and claimed so completely by all the Abrahamic Faiths. She is Judaic, Christian and Islamic. She belongs to Ethiopia, to Southern Arabia and to Jerusalem.

What are the three legends? We know the bare bones of the Christian legend. The second comes from the Koran. The Koran introduces us to a different legend. In the Old Testament, she comes to Solomon a Pagan Queen and leaves a Pagan Queen. In the Koran, she arrives as a Pagan Queen and leaves a follower of Allah. In Ethiopia... the whole story of Ethiopia revolves around the Queen of Sheba.

The Old Testament is where my quest began so this is where I look for her first. There is an art gallery in Mayfair, London, behind the Royal Academy which is dedicated to Ethiopian religious icons. I ring the bell and enter into the crypt-like space. Here are depictions of founding saints and Church fathers but also something more talismanic, mysterious, scrawled in red and black, banishing demons, calling up the secret names of God.

The Queen of Sheba sits between the pagan worship of planets, zodiacs, spirits, and the Old Testament assertion of God. It is intriguing and strange to me. I ask the gallery owner where I can learn more about this subject, and he hands me a name. Eyob Derillo, the British Library. Underneath is scrawled an email address. I write immediately and check my phone for replies.

After a few days, one comes. Eyob Derillo is polite and reserved. He does not know a great deal about the Queen of Sheba but he certainly knows about ancient Christianity. He works with religious illuminated manuscripts at the British Library. Would I like to look at some?

It is two tube stops from the BBC and I am there as the library opens, joining the queue of students and academics in front of the unremarkable modern red brick building, which nevertheless holds the weight of history in millions of books. Inside I look round for Eyob among the stream of international faces, absorbed by their own intellectual journeys.

A tall, athletic figure approaches, broad shoulders, wide-set features, a willing handshake and an unfolding luminous smile. It is Eyob.

I ask him if there is anything I can find out here about the Queen of Sheba and he urges patience. First, he can show me some bibles. In a dimly lit room, he lifts in the tender manner of a midwife, illuminated sacred texts from within cabinets.

Eyob catalogues and digitises ancient manuscripts. He imaginatively exists in the early mountain monasteries, in the world of angels and mystics. His special interest is in the occult knowledge of the early monks. He takes me via the bookshop to show me with wry pride his chapter on magic spells in a book about Harry Potter.

The story of the Queen of Sheba is known to him from the Old Testament and the Koran but is loved by him for its association with Ethiopia. In the national book of Ethiopia, *The Kebra Nagast*, the Queen of Sheba gave birth to the kingdom. Sheba or Saba is Ethiopia.

Eyob looks out a handsome version of the King James's bible and we sit at a low table together poring over the thirteen verses that remain our text.

1. And when the queen of Sheba heard of the fame of Solomon concerning the name of the Lord, she came to prove him with hard questions.
2. And she came to Jerusalem with a very great train, with camels that bare spices, and very much gold, and precious stones: and when she came to Solomon, she communed with him of all that was in her heart.

3. And Solomon told her all her questions: there was not anything hidden from the king, which he told her not.
4. And when the queen of Sheba had seen all Solomon's wisdom, and the house that he had built.
5. And the meat of his table, and the sitting of his servants, and the attendance of his ministers, and their apparel, and his cupbearers, and his ascent by which he went up unto the house of the Lord; there was no more spirit in her.
6. And she said to the king, It was a true report that I heard in mine own land of thy acts and of thy wisdom.
7. Howbeit I believed not the words until I came, and my eyes had seen it: and, behold, the half was not told me: thy wisdom and prosperity exceedeth the fame which I heard.
8. Happy are thy men, happy are these thy servants, which stand continually before thee, and that hear thy wisdom.
9. Blessed be the Lord thy God, which delighted in thee, to set thee on the throne of Israel: because the Lord loved Israel forever, therefore made he thee king, to do judgment and justice.
10. And she gave the king a hundred and twenty talents of gold, and of spices very great store, and precious stones: there came no more such abundance of spices as these which the queen of Sheba gave to King Solomon.
11. And the navy also of Hiram, that brought gold from Ophir, brought in from Ophir great plenty of almug trees, and precious stones.
12. And the king made of the almug trees pillars for the house of the Lord, and for the king's house, harps also and psalteries for singers: there came no such almug trees, nor were seen unto this day.
13. And King Solomon gave unto the Queen of Sheba all her desire, whatsoever she asked, beside that which Solomon gave her of his royal bounty. So she turned and went to her own country, she and her servants.

What is the message of the thirteen verses? I concentrate on the first verse. The Queen of Sheba came to witness Solomon and to test him with hard questions.

Eyob likes the last verse.

Solomon gave the Queen of Sheba what she desired and she returned to her own country. This is where her story really begins, according to Ethiopia.

Eyob's supervisor is looking at him across the room. He is wondering what Eyob might be doing with a journalist. I pack up my notebook, furtively. The Queen of Sheba will be our 3,000-year-old scoop.

Eyob asks if I have visited Canterbury Cathedral. I tell him, a trifle dismissively, that of course, I have my brother was a choirboy there, I know it well.

"So you have seen the Queen of Sheba windows there?"

I haven't. Sometimes we only see things when we know what we are looking for. I shall have to become much more observant if I am to tackle the mystery of the Queen of Sheba.

"What do the windows show?" I ask.

"I don't know, you have to see for yourself," he says. "But there is one thing that interests me. In Canterbury Cathedral, the Queen of Sheba is white. But in Cologne Cathedral she is black. Why is that?"

If I am searching for Old Testament truths, the great cathedrals of Europe must contain clues.

Canterbury Cathedral, England, has its roots in the eleventh century. Cologne is the soaring gothic landmark built in the thirteen century.

On a crisp April day, I catch the train from London St Pancras, next to the British Library, to Canterbury. This is the route of the Eurostar to Europe and feels fast and international but the old road to Canterbury was in the Middle Ages worn down by pilgrims. Still, they come along Pilgrim's Way, the ancient track along the way North Downs, leading finally to the shrine of Thomas Becket.

The fourteenth-century Canterbury Tales, by Geoffrey Chaucer, based on a group of pilgrims entertaining each other with stories on their journey to Canterbury, is still studied by school children amazed that language of the period can be so bawdy. The Wife of Bath's tale is a dash of feminism in an age of Patriarchy, a critique by a serially married, sexually experienced and frank woman, of the double moral standards of men and women. Why are women defined only in their relations to men? Wife, mother, daughter, sister.

The tale has at its centre a riddle: a knight who rapes a maiden will escape punishment if he can find out what it is that women desire. The answer, he discovers, is sovereignty. The theme of bold women is embedded in this journey.

But while the Wife of Bath was a worldly figure, the Queen of Sheba has a foot in the heavens. She is a pivotal religious figure, a bridge between the Old and New Testaments, ready for the Day of Judgement. It is quite a religious transformation for a pagan queen, a woman we believe would have worshipped Al-maqah, the Saba moon god.

The Queen of Sheba's influence spread through the Jewish, Christian and Islamic faith. She forms the founding dynasty of Ethiopia, for all the country's leaders are said to be descended from Solomon.

From these religious foundations, her reputation carries across the Middle East and into Europe through artistic imagination and folklore.

We choose the faith with which we feel at home and Canterbury Cathedral is familiar to me. My elder brother was a soloist here. He used to scare me by showing me the cracked paving stone in the cloister, which he claimed was the result of an unhappy ghost named Nell Cook. He also awed me a little with his top Cs. The choirboys were careless about their gift, playing cards in between tumbling into the pews for Christmas carols. They took bets on who would faint first during the Good Friday six-hour service.

The Dean of Canterbury is Robert Willis. I find him at the Dean's house, in a walled garden bathed in sunshine, with wide borders of budding summer roses. We drink iced water at a slightly unstable table and he points to the choir's house down the path.

Dr Willis, who composes hymns, understands the power of storytelling.

He has thick grey hair, full rosy lips, and a peaceful manner tinged with mischief. He recalls the former Archbishop of Canterbury, Rowan Williams, an erudite and holy man considered regarded as a little opaque by the media. But what he understood was stories.

Rowan Williams once phoned the Dean about a forthcoming sermon and said he had decided to talk about the C. S. Lewis *Chronicles of Narnia* books instead. He wanted to talk about the figure of Aslan the lion as a way of illustrating the 'large interior' versus the 'limited exterior'. Stories are a way of discussing large truths.

The Dean sees the Queen of Sheba in this light. She is a figure that leads us to large truths. We walk across the cloisters to the north aisle to look at the stained glass portrait of the Queen of Sheba. It is smaller and more beautiful than I expected. Dr Willis says that the windows speak at different times of day in different lights, constantly altering perceptions.

Next to the window, a restoration of a great organ is taking place and a carpenter stops work to listen to the Dean. The bible windows are incomplete, but they show scenes from the Old Testament, fulfilled by the New Testament.

The Queen of Sheba is both a human and a theological sign. She has journeyed to see the splendour of King Solomon and all her questions are answered.

What strikes the Dean is the modern human form of the Queen of Sheba. She is shapely, the folds of her dress draped over a sinuous form. "And see how she is raising her hands to Solomon, very expressively, as if to say: 'Oh my'."

This scene is juxtaposed with a window showing the adoration of the Magi, bringing gifts of gold, myrrh and frankincense to the baby Jesus. Kings have come to ask questions, and so they travel naturally to the source of power. They go to see King Herod. But he does not have the answers. They have mistaken earthly power for eternal power. They seek answers from a baby who cannot speak, but who has the answers.

The notion of power in Christianity is revolutionary. The meek shall inherit the earth. It is harder for a rich man to enter heaven than a camel to go through the eye of a needle. The Queen of Sheba is a tale of wealth and glory, which finds its sequel in the story of Mary and Jesus. No gold in sight, just a stable.

The Dean also cites Jesus at the Sea of Galilee, prophesying that the Queen of the South will return. The sea journey is a theological one. Water is significant. I'm interested in this because I have been thinking about the Queen of Sheba's great journey to meet Solomon, and whether she would have travelled by land or by sea.

The Dean says: "Look at Noah's Ark. From water comes salvation. Look at St John."

After the resurrection, Jesus appears across the Sea of Galilee and says: "Cast your net, go fishing. It is the narrative of creation. Life came from the sea."

"All faiths," says the dean, "are aligned in the notion of the journey to wisdom. It is a pilgrimage. I say this to pilgrims who come to Canterbury Cathedral. You will return and it is when you are through the door and reflect that you see what you have learned."

"What are the obstacles to wisdom? The kings got it wrong! They went to the obvious centre of power and wealth seeking wisdom. These are just symbols. Astrophysicists will tell you this. Stephen Hawking got nearer to the gospel of St Mark. Wisdom is never complete. The journey is never complete."

How does it compare with Cologne cathedral? I undertake this leg of the journey soon after my trip to Canterbury. I am going to look at her depiction in three windows at Cologne Cathedral, described in Germany as 'the most sublime monument of church architecture in our fatherland'.

Here, she represents prophecy and radiance. The cathedral itself is a monument to light above darkness.

The two Gothic spires are the first thing you see from the air as Cologne comes into view, near to the River Rhine, mighty and ancient in an otherwise unremarkable city. There is the tragic reason for the city's lack of architectural charm. Cologne was one of the chief bombing targets during the Second World War.

In the first window in which she appears, she is a tall, white queen wearing a crown and bearing treasures for Solomon on his throne. He accepts the gifts as his due. The next window, on the right, is of Mary and her baby Jesus. Resplendent kings approach her, representing, according to my guide, Europe, Africa and Asia. The bible windows, as in Canterbury Cathedral, juxtapose the Queen of Sheba with the nativity.

She comes seeking wisdom and glory. It is a prophetic act, foreseeing The Three Wise Men also coming for answers. Indeed the metaphor is so exact that some theological scholars believe that Solomon is no more historically real than the Queen of Sheba. Her reason for journeying to see him is an act of religious worship. Solomon represents divinity.

The second bible window in which the Queen of Sheba is portrayed in Cologne Cathedral is in the oldest medieval part. It is the oldest thirteenth-century glass painting. The bible windows are typological again, matching ten events from Jesus's life, with those of the Old Testament. The cross of Jesus unifies all the pictures as the tree of life. The creation of Eve, from Adam's rib, becomes the birth of Mary. Moses and the burning bush becomes the birth of Christ.

The Queen of Sheba, approaching Solomon, becomes the Adoration of the Magi. Finally, Mary is enthroned and Christ is the judge of the world. The two parts of the bible are united. There is a striking difference between this older depiction of the Queen of Sheba and the first picture. The pose is similar, but this time the Queen of Sheba is black. Why did a later century whitewash her?

There is a third portrait of the Queen of Sheba in this cathedral, in what is called the younger bible chapel window. This was brought from a Dominican Church. Here, she is black and standing apart rather than worshipping Solomon. She has a crown, as he does. The colours are glorious, crimson, gold, kingfisher blues, turquoise green. The intensity of the colours, dance in front of your eyes even as you leave the cathedral.

As I look back at the spires of Cologne, from the air, I am pleased to think of the Queen of Sheba being an integral part of the Adoration of the Magi, a creation of the frankincense trade, a traveller who saw that wisdom exceeded even glory. The stained glass windows of Cologne Cathedral are a glimpse of imagined Jerusalem and the prize the Queen of Sheba might have discovered there. The medieval origins of Canterbury and of Cologne explain the interest in the Queen: they were built in a period that developed an obsession with her.

The Medieval period was full of quests. Now I have mine. I want to find out what the Queen of Sheba was searching for, and why men and history, often the same thing, feared her cleverness so much.

This sets my quest in perspective. We are all on a journey. The next state of mine will be to Cambridge to visit the former Archbishop of Canterbury we have talked about today, Rowan Williams, and find out what are the larger truths he thinks the Queen of Sheba represents.

It's not too fanciful to imagine the Queen of Sheba in the setting of an Oxbridge college. The point of university education is to ask Hard Questions. Perhaps one of the world's oldest universities would be a good setting to try to understand her. It is a mellow, warm day and Cambridge is looking irresistible. I walk along The Backs, by the lovely stretch of River Cam that flows past a group of the town's most handsome colleges. The punts are out on the clear river, the grey stone soaked in sunlight; there are manicured lawns and afternoon shadows, meadow grass threaded with poppies and cornflowers, beech trees showing that early-season emerald. It is a garden of delight. I walk through the visitor throngs and past the tourist shops to Magdalene College.

Dr Williams, having retired from his post as archbishop, is Master of Magdalene. He greets me at the door of the Master's Lodge and we go out to sit in the garden. His long white beard and quiet, sonorous voice enhance the impression that he has a foot in the spiritual as well as the temporal world and might disappear at any moment.

This is what he said about the visit of the Queen of Sheba. "She was there to burnish the glory of Solomon." This is all he says. He asks me to report back to him when I have made the journey.

Is that it? She's in the Bible purely as a means of demonstrating the glory of Solomon? Is that what women are for, to exclaim the magnificence of men?

"Oh my!"

The Queen of Sheba arrived, witnessed the glory of Solomon and left. And yet she far exceeds her cameo role. In the creation of fables that were conjured and expanded, told and retold across the African, Arab and European worlds, the religious importance of the Queen has taken on an epic quality that has seen her equal and even eclipses her consort. As her legend grows, she stretches back to Eve and forwards to Mary. She is embedded in the greatest religious myths, she inspires the Crusades, she is enthroned in Jerusalem, she sits at Judgment Day. She is there at Creation and at Armageddon. Her significance rises in the Medieval Christian world as she becomes a proxy for Jerusalem.

Indeed, in the New Testament, Matthew, Gospels 12, reports Jesus investing her with far more significance than the king: "On Judgment Day, the Queen of the South will rise up with this generation and condemn it because she came from the ends of the earth to hear the Wisdom of Solomon and there is something greater than Solomon here."

Before we examine those wider stories, let us look at the Koranic account of her visit to Solomon. In the Koran, the point of the Queen of Sheba's visit to Solomon—or Suleiman or Salayman; the prophet—is to give up the deities in which she believes in favour of Allah. I read the relevant passages and find that her display of wealth is slightly frowned on: Suleiman does not want her treasure.

This account has become woven with colourful storytelling. There is a description of Solomon's army of men, birds and Jinns, or spirits. In later traditions, the Jinns become the genies of the Arabian nights. Solomon sees that his favourite hoopoe bird is missing and finds that the bird has been travelling in the land of Saba. The hoopoe bird reports: "I come to you from Sheba with sure news. I found a woman ruling over the people, she has been given many blessings and has a mighty throne! I found her and her people worshipping the sun instead of Allah."

Solomon minds about the false gods, rather than desiring the Queen's wealth and sends the bird back: "Soon shall we see whether thou has told the truth or lied! Go thou with this letter of mine, and deliver it to them."

The Queen of Sheba—or Bilqis as she is in the Koran—receives the letter: "Ye chiefs! Here is delivered to me a letter worthy of respect. It is from Solomon and is as follows: 'In the name of Allah, most gracious, most merciful. Be ye not arrogant against me, but come to me in submission to the true religion'."

She was suspicious that Solomon wanted to invade her kingdom, so she sent him gifts—diplomacy rather than warfare being her statecraft. Suleiman in the Koran has no appetite for gifts of treasure. "Will ye give me abundance in wealth? But that which Allah has given me is better than that which He has given you."

When Bilqis arrives she finds Solomon's jinns have transported her throne, which is waiting for her. "So when she arrived, she was asked: 'Is this thy throne?' She said: 'It seems the same. And knowledge was bestowed on us in advance of this and we have submitted to Allah (in Islam)'."

There follows an account of her walk across the palace, which is embellished and darkened in medieval folklore. In the Koran, it is curious. The floor is made of shimmering glass, which looks like water. The queen therefore lifts her skirts so that she does not get wet. The ending is a declaration of faith in Islam. Bilqis cries: "Oh my Lord! I have indeed wronged my soul: I do (now) submit (in Islam) with Solomon, to the Lord of the Worlds."

What is the significance of the glass floor? The interpretations differ. The queen of Sheba has come in search of wisdom. Is the lesson here on the dangers of deception? That appearances are not what they seem? She is urged in the Koran to put behind her beliefs in deities, the sun and moon gods.

To try to get to the bottom of this, I return to Cambridge, this time to visit the Shaykh Zayed, Lecturer in Islamic Studies at the university's Faculty of Divinity. We meet at the Cambridge Muslim College, a former Victorian vicarage, close to the Botanical Gardens. It is a handsome redbrick building designed by the great church architect Sir George Gilbert Scott.

The Sunni Muslim lecturer is Tim Winter or Shaykh Abdel Hakim Murad. I worked with Tim's brother Henry, a very successful football writer when I was at the Daily Telegraph years ago. The brothers have large, pale blue eyes, but there the resemblance ends. Henry was always convivial, Tim looks serious and devout. He fetches the Koran from his bookshelf and studies the passage about the Queen of Sheba in silence. We are agreed: the difference between the Koran and the Bible is that she submits to Suleiman's God of Allah.

Tim Winter explains that it is of central importance that she is a pagan Queen. Like Rowan Williams, he does not elaborate more on a central truth. The implication is that it is up to me to find out the rest. It is my quest, my journey. Nobody is going to furnish me with the answers; I must return with them myself.

So what is the evidence for that pagan belief? Well, in the sanctuary of Meqaber Gaewa, near Wukro, Ethiopia, there was a single podium temple with a portico and staircase. The most striking of these is a limestone statue of a female figure, in a full-length decorated robe, sitting on a throne. Her head is missing; her body is balanced and confident. She is holding two scrolls and her seat is on a raised podium, which is Sabaean iconography. The inscription reads:

"Almaqah [the moon god], may he grant the blessing of (male) offspring." A pagan female ruler, who gives birth to a son. Could this have been an inspiration for the Queen of Sheba, a pagan queen who needed to be converted with the advent of Judaic then Christian and then Islamic faith?

Cults of the sun existed everywhere in Mesopotamia and Egypt. A seal found at Jerusalem in a tomb dating from seventh century BC shows a solar god flanked by two minor gods: Righteousness and Justice. The Queen of Sheba worshipped the sun. Was her coupling with Solomon a submission of pagan to monotheism or did she have her own force?

The conversion is clearly laid out in the Koran. These are the verses picking up here from the moment Solomon carries out a roll call of the animals and realises that the hoopoe bird is not there:

14. Then he inspected the birds, and said, "Why do I not see the hoopoe? Or is he among the absentees?
15. "I will punish him most severely, or slay him, unless he gives me a valid excuse."
16. But he did not stay for long. He said, "I have learnt something you did not know. I have come to you from Sheba, with reliable information.
17. "I found a woman ruling over them, and she was given of everything, and she has a magnificent throne.
18. "I found her and her people worshipping the sun, instead of God. Satan made their conduct appear good to them and diverted them from the path, so they are not guided.
19. "If only they would worship God, who brings to light the mysteries of the heavens and the earth, and knows what you conceal and what you reveal.
20. "God—There is no god but He, the Lord of the Sublime Throne."
21. He said, "We will see, whether you have spoken the truth, or whether you are a liar.
22. "Go with this letter of mine, and deliver it to them; then withdraw from them, and see how they respond."
23. She said, "O Counsellors, a gracious letter was delivered to me.
24. "It is from Solomon, and it is, 'In the Name of God, the Gracious, the Merciful.
25. "Do not defy me, and come to me submissively'."

26. She said, "O counsellors, advise me in this matter of mine. I never make a decision unless you are present."
27. They said, "We are a people of might and great courage, but the decision is yours, so consider what you wish to command."
28. She said, "When kings enter a city, they devastate it, and subjugate its dignified people. Thus they always do.
29. "I am sending them a gift, and will see what the envoys bring back."
30. When he came to Solomon, he said, "Are you supplying me with money? What God has given me is better than what He has given you. It is you who delight in your gift.
31. "Go back to them. We will come upon them with troops they cannot resist; and we will expel them from there, disgraced and humiliated."
32. He said, "O notables, which one of you will bring me her throne before they come to me in submission?"
33. An imp of the sprites said, "I will bring it to you before you rise from your seat. I am strong and reliable enough to do it."
34. He who had knowledge from the book said, "I will bring it to you before your glance returns to you." And when he saw it settled before him, he said, "This is from the grace of my Lord, to test me, whether I am grateful or ungrateful. He who is grateful, his gratitude is to his own credit; but he who is ungrateful—my Lord is Independent and Generous."
35. He said, "Disguise her throne for her, and we shall see whether she will be guided, or remains one of the misguided."
36. When she arrived, it was said, "Is your throne like this?" She said, "As if this is it." "We were given knowledge before her, and we were submissive."
37. But she was prevented by what she worshipped besides God; she belonged to a disbelieving people.
38. It was said to her, "Go inside the palace." And when she saw it, she thought it was a deep pond, and she bared her legs. He said, "It is a palace paved with glass." She said, "My Lord, I have done wrong to myself, and I have submitted with Solomon, to God, Lord of the Worlds."

There is a much greater sense of equality in the Bible version. In the Koran, she sounds pretty nervous about making the trip, she's on the receiving end of the question—the test of recognising the disguised throne that Solomon has had one of his jinns fly in—and she converts rapidly from her worship of the sun to Allah. She also meets an indifference to her material wealth. She witnesses what money cannot buy.

Why was Solomon so important? What made him a prophet to Jews and to Muslims? His dates are usually given as around 970 to 931 BC. He had succeeded his father David as King of Israel. The Hebrew Bible, the basis of the Old Testament, records him as the builder of the First Temple in Jerusalem. He has become eternally associated with wisdom, thanks to a dream in which, asked by God what he wanted, he suggested wisdom rather than giving the kind of long life, riches, happiness answer that normally follows such a question.

The most popular example of his wisdom was his judgment when two women claimed to be the mother of the same child. He is said to have ordered the child to be cut in two and shared between them: the mother who said she would rather hand the child to the other than see it killed was declared the mother and awarded custody because she had shown such superior maternal love.

Later, he rather blotted his copybook by conducting affairs with foreign women and worshipping other gods. He is said to have had 700 wives and 300 concubines, which I worry puts his affair with the Queen of Sheba in a different light—and doesn't necessarily do her credit.

For the Ethiopians, the Queen was also too flesh and blood to be myth or allegory. The Queen of Sheba of *The Kebra Nagast* is every inch a woman, living breathing, fecund flesh and blood:

"And the Queen departed and came into the country of Bâlâ Zadîsârĕya nine months and five days after she had separated from King Solomon. And the pains of childbirth laid hold upon her, and she brought forth a man child, and she gave it to the nurse with great pride and delight.

"And she tarried until the days of her purification were ended, and then she came to her own country with great pomp and ceremony. And her officers who had remained there brought gifts to their mistress, and made obeisance to her, and did homage to her, and all the borders of the country rejoiced at her coming. Those who were nobles among them she arrayed in splendid apparel, and to some, she gave gold and silver, and hyacinthine and purple robes, and she gave them all manner of things that could be desired. And she ordered her kingdom aright, and none disobeyed her command; for she loved wisdom and God strengthened her kingdom."

The child was her son Menelik I, who brought the Ark of the Covenant to Axum—there's some dispute over whether he stole it, or swapped it for the copy his father Solomon had given him as protection—and founded an Ethiopian monarchy that reigned for almost 3,000 years. Solomon's Egyptian wife—the relationship with the Queen of Sheba was by no means an exclusive one—took it badly, according to *The Kebra Nagast*.

"Thy son hath carried away thy Lady Zion, thy son whom thou hast begot, who springeth from an alien people into which God hath not commanded you to marry, that is to say, from an Ethiopian woman, who is not of thy colour, and is not akin to thy country, and who is, moreover, black."

From her origins in those core texts, the Queen of Sheba is richly written into Christian myths and Arab and Islamic storytelling. Through her son Menelik, she is responsible for faith in Ethiopia. She has become an embodiment of Jerusalem, which is why she is there at the end, wrapped in the gold of Ophir, a prophetess, a possible Queen of heaven, and a figure of divine judgement.

The notion was expanded by the English Benedictine monk, the Venerable Bede, in the eighth century AD, who suggested that the Queen of Sheba and Jesus would rule together, quoting Psalm 45: "On your right hand stands the Queen, in gold from Ophir."

She is even more intimately involved with Jesus in the story of the True Cross—much developed and embroidered in medieval times—the account of the origins of the wood that was eventually to become the cross on which Christ was crucified. Different versions of the story have the wood coming from trees that grew either from seeds Adam ate before his death or which were planted in his mouth after his death. Another account suggests the tree came from a part of the Tree of Knowledge, in the Garden of Eden.

The tree is sent for use as one of the timbers of the temple built by Solomon in Jerusalem but is used instead as a bridge over a stream. The Queen of Sheba happens on it as she goes to meet Solomon, falls in prayer before it and—in a flash of visionary power—warns the king that the wood will have great significance for the future of the Jews. He listens, or doesn't, depending on the version of the story. He looks after the wood or discards it. Eventually, it is taken up—generations later—and used to construct the cross.

Returning from Canterbury and Cologne, I message Eyob. I know now about the Old Testament Queen of Sheba who asked hard questions and left satisfied. I know about her conversion from pagan queen to a disciple of Allah in the Koran. And I am starting to assemble the folklore of the middle ages of religious myths.

But it is *The Kebra Nagast*—the Glory of Kings—that is the most vivid version of her of all. Eyob meets me at St Pancras hotel lobby, shaking raindrops from his hair and a copy of *The Kebra Nagast* in his pocket.

The reason that Eyob cared more about the departure of the Queen of Sheba than her arrival was that she founded the royal dynasty of Ethiopia, through her son Menelik. And he brought the Ark of the Covenant to Axum.

For medieval Christians throughout Europe, these matters were real rather than fantastical. There are different theories on what happened to the Ark of the Covenant after it disappeared from Solomon's Temple. The seventeenth-century Dutch Jewish philosopher Baruch Spinoza wrote in *Tractatus Theologico-Politicus* that he found it "strange that scripture tells us nothing of what became of the Ark of the Covenant; but there can be no doubt that it perished or was burnt along with the temple."

Others claim the Ark lies under the Temple Mount in Jerusalem in secret, that High Priest Uzzi hid it in Mount Gerizim; it was taken to Arabia in the days of the Jurham, lords of Mecca; the prophet Jeremiah concealed it in a cave or took it to Ireland where it became the palladium of the High Kings of Tara.

But in Ethiopia, from the time of King Lalibela, in the twelfth century, the Ethiopians have been certain. You only need to touch the earth of Ethiopia to feel the devout nature of the place: a deep Christian faith bound up with older truths and legend. It is not only the Wisdom of Solomon, the construction of Solomon's Temple and the return to Ethiopia of Menelik.

There are more signs. When Herod ordered the death of new-borns, Mary and Joseph fled to Egypt and were led, by a pillar of light, to Ethiopia. The marks of the feet of Christ are to be seen at the rock of Tana Kirqos. A covenant exists between Mary and Ethiopia.

The Queen of Sheba's connections are ancient and deep. Three faiths, three legends, a mystery of the Middle East.

Back in the manicured lawn of my Norfolk garden, I ponder her blazing trail. She is so distant from my life here. I walk along the herbaceous border picking out weeds sprouting between the paintbox coloured anemones and opening irises. I have been neglecting the maintenance of my life here.

It is pleasant and ordered, full of boundaries. A kitchen garden ending with a row of yew trees. A barn owl nests in a box that I have put up to coax him to settle here.

But my thoughts are with the gold-encrusted Queen of the South.

I re-read a passage in *The Kebra Nagast* in which her splendour is defined: "And the Queen of the South of whom He spake was the Queen of Ethiopia. And in the words 'ends of the earth' [He maketh allusion] to the delicacy of the constitution of women, and the long distance of the journey, and the burning heat of the sun, and the hunger on the way, and the thirst for water.

"And this Queen of the South was very beautiful in face, and her stature was superb, and her understanding and intelligence, which God had given her, were of such high character that she went to Jerusalem to hear the Wisdom of Solomon; now this was done by the command of God and it was His good pleasure.

"And moreover, she was exceedingly rich, for God had given her glory, and riches, and gold, and silver, and splendid apparel, and camels, and slaves, and trading men (or, merchants). And they carried on her business and trafficked for her by sea and by land..."

The sheer ambition of the story hits me. The Queen arrives by sea and land— I imagine her in a golden vessel, a thousand years before Cleopatra. But she has a self-possession missing in Cleopatra. The Queen of Sheba is a religious icon as well as the queen of flesh. She is sacred as well as gorgeous. She is beyond our touch. She comes to find the deepest secrets of faith in the holy land. Then her religious persona divides. Either she submits to the knowledge that she has acquired, or she returns to her land of Ethiopia and takes the knowledge back with her. She leaves behind Solomon.

It is a great love affair with does not last. The legacy of it is her son. As the weak early summer sun sinks low over the yew trees I shiver and pull on a cardigan. I am thinking of my own first love affair, in a city that celebrated the Queen of Sheba through the religion of art.

I have a memory of a portrait of her by the Italian artist Piero della Francesca. It was of the Legend of the Cross—the arc of the religious story. The Queen of Sheba saw how the story would end. If I am to trace the journey of the Queen of Sheba I must find the emotional heart of it. I will return to Florence, where I loved and lost my youthful husband but kept his son. The present is created in the past.

Chapter 3
Florence, May Memories of a Past Love

I am going to delve into my own past to imagine the passion between Solomon and the Queen of Sheba. We do not know how old the Queen of Sheba was when she set off for Jerusalem, although we do know that she was established as a stateswoman and appears as a woman of substance rather than as an ingénue.

But here is something: she had a love affair, then parted and lived the rest of her life separately. She went to witness fame and glory but returned to her son to form a different axis.

I can understand a fraction of this. I was briefly married to a British actor, Julian Sands, and I have a beloved son by him, in his thirties. When I think of Julian I remember the spires and bridges of Florence where we were both intensely united and unknowingly close to separation. I was twenty-four years old, and Julian was 26.

He was appearing in a film of the EM Forster novel *Room with a View*. We were newly married, it was summer, and I was pregnant with our son. I flew out to join him in Florence. We stayed at the splendid hotel Excelsior where the other actors in the film, who included Daniel Day-Lewis, Helena Bonham Carter were companions. There were nightly banquets and my husband I would then wander through the cobbled street for late opening ice cream parlours. Hollywood is the closest I have seen to a contemporary court of King Solomon.

During the day, I would visit the profusion of churches; whichever square I turned into another would be waiting. I became lost among them but miraculously ended up back at the hotel. I would sit on the wooden pews to avoid the midday sun and to stroke my stomach, trying to imagine the journey ahead for both of us.

I was surprised how many other people reached out to do the same, bending to admire and touch my stomach as if it had magical properties. I realised then the sacred state of maternity in this Catholic city and the revered role of Mary.

Even while I explored this city of the Madonna, I felt the relationship with my unborn son grow stronger and the bonds with my husband weaken. Julian was pulled by the magnet of Hollywood; there were too many treasures on offer to him to settle for a wife and a child. Our marriage ended the following year in another Italian Renaissance city, Venice. He told me that he had decided to emigrate to Los Angeles: and I must now make my choice. LA was not my place, nor my choice.

When I awoke the next day in Venice, Julian was gone. I gave my wedding ring to the boatman in payment to get to the airport, and returned home to London. I arrived home late at night and crept up the stairs to lift my sleepy son from his cot. He put his warm dewy damp arms around my neck. One journey ends, another begins.

Almost forty years later I am preparing to return to Florence. I want to go back to the ornate Baptistery at the Duomo, to look again at the scene of Solomon's meeting with the Queen of Sheba that features among the Old Testament images decorating the fifteenth-century doors.

I arrange to meet Matthias, a Renaissance historian, because what else would you want to be in Florence?

Unfortunately, an hour or so before I am due to land at one of the world's most beautiful and historical cities, I am walking instead into the arrivals lounge of Southend Airport, on the Essex coast. Our plane has been diverted because of an engine failure. I text Matthias the historian to tell him I shall be unable to appear in the afternoon.

He texts straight back: "It seems perfectly corresponding to the chimera aspect of the Queen of Sheba."

There's a moment in any airport delay when a sixth sense tells you your plane is not going to fly. A harassed airline official suggests a replacement plane will soon be on its way from Dublin. Or—and here she gives the game away—perhaps we will be put on coaches and taken back to City Airport, London. I notice there is a cheap, alternative flight leaving from Gatwick in three hours and rushing for the station to leap on trains to and then out of London. I fly into Pisa, ring to stop my pension locking the front door for the night, take a taxi down the dark autostrada and am tucked up in bed by 11:00 p.m. I feel the Queen of Sheba would have approved. Sometimes it is easier to arrive than to travel.

Matthias and I do get to meet at the Baptistery, where we examine the 'the Gates of Paradise', the name given in tribute by Michelangelo to the astonishingly detailed brass doors created by the sculptor and goldsmith Lorenzo

Ghiberti between 1425 and 1452. We are actually looking at perfect copies, the originals having been removed for safe keeping. The artist created a series of Old Testament scenes, including Adam and Eve and Moses receiving the Ten Commandments. Matthias points to the figures of Solomon and Sheba in profile, in front of a nave opening into a dome and choir chapel. Ghiberti appears to have modelled Solomon's Temple on the Duomo. The Queen of Sheba comes from the left, a sign of Christian approach and her arm is across her chest in a further gesture of humility. Her head is slightly bowed.

The Queen of Sheba I had looked at in the roundel window at Canterbury Cathedral expressed open to joy and marvel. The Queen here appears more ceremonial. Her hand is touched by Solomon, who is a stout, bearded figure of age and consequence. They stand at equal height and this looks like the union of marriage.

My fleeting husband Julian and I stood in front of this door—there were no selfies in those days, and I have only a handful of photographs of our time together. The lack of documentation does not mean that we were not there nor that we did not love each other for a brief period. I bear this in mind when questioning the existence of the queen of Sheba because of the lack of historical texts.

The queen on the Baptistery door is bare-headed, a sign of Christian worship queen. She has the oval face and straight nose of Renaissance western beauty, but behind her are three women of more African aspect and costume. One holds the queen's crown and headdress on a cushion in a scene reminiscent of the Adoration of the Magi. The courtiers on her side of the three-dimensional frieze look livelier than Solomon's court on the right. Horses jostle with figures, there are beasts and there is a bird on the far left, which could be a hoopoe, though it looks more like a bird of prey. On the right, there is a man with a monkey on his shoulder.

The scene is balanced by the architecture of columns and arches behind the central figures and by the crowd scenes: figures look out of windows, top left and top right of the frieze. It is a scene of symmetry and harmony, which I am beginning to associate with Solomon and Sheba. It is both realistic and symbolic.

Matthias notes that the scene at the Florence Baptistery was sculpted at a time the Catholic Church was seeking new relations with the orthodox eastern churches, partly under the threat of the increasing influence of Turkey and the Muslim world. The churches had begun conferring at Ferrara in 1438 and moved to Florence when the plague arrived in Ferrara. The conference went on until

1445 as the eastern and western churches sought common ground: this is what Solomon and Sheba symbolise in these early Renaissance years.

More than a century later, she is re-invented again. Paolo Veronese, the sumptuous Venetian painter, captures her in 1584 in a scene in which she offers gifts to Solomon. He is perched on his throne looking slightly fastidious. She is buxom in brocade, with her African entourage, passing up gift after gift. The architecture of the Temple looks slightly Roman, and a window reveals an Italian looking landscape of blue sky and cypress trees. This is the picture that the English Victorian critic John Ruskin cited as his reason for abandoning the evangelical Protestant church tradition in which he had grown up.

In his autobiography *Praeterita*, he writes of his life-changing visit in 1858 to see The Queen of Sheba Offering Gifts to Solomon in Turin. Before this day he had been a dutiful, church-going Protestant. Indeed, he had been to service shortly before entering the gallery.

The Queen and her retinue, opulent and fruitful, "glowed in the full afternoon light."

Suffused with the colour and pleasure of the painting he realised "that things done delightfully and rightly were always done by the help and in the Spirit of God." On that day, "my evangelical beliefs were put away, to be debated of no more." In a letter to a friend, Ruskin relayed his newfound wisdom: that "to be a first-rate painter, you mustn't be pious—but rather a little wicked and entirely a man of the world." O there you have it: The Queen of Sheba as an ocean-going femme fatale.

In Renaissance Florence, the Queen of Sheba is a religious, ritualised figure of solemnity and dignity. In Venice, she is opulent and earthly. There is a greater sense of drama and movement and the setting becomes elaborate. Matthias says the Queen of Sheba comes to represent Venice itself, a symbol of trade wealth. Religious significance, commercial significance: the two tropes of the Queen of Sheba.

Veronese's contemporary, Tintoretto, also painted the Queen of Sheba. In his painting, dated around 1545, she is a little more queenly, with an entourage of women in high headdresses. It is also exotic. An oriental figure lies in front of her. The architectural columns are classical and by the water. Jerusalem, landlocked, looks very like Venice. The Queen of Sheba seems to have sailed into the harbour, just as she was leaving a harbour in Claude Lorrain's painting, just over a century later. What is the Renaissance ideal of beauty? It would be Botticelli's Venus. The Queen of Sheba was not permitted to be black. Yet in the stained glass of Cologne Cathedral, around 1507–25 or so years after Venus—she was.

Memories are flooding back for me. It is curious to think of my younger self-standing in this exact same spot looking at the Queen of Sheba panels. I could not imagine what lay ahead: The Queen of Sheba could. She had a sense of composure and of destiny. She was not afraid.

Her gift of foresight—of calamity and then redemption in the New Testament makes her more compelling to follow. She knows what I will discover.

The artist who captured her prophetic nature was Piero Della Francesca. His great works are guarded in Arezzo, about forty miles across Tuscany. I have made this journey before. Last time it was because I was told pregnant women were blessed in Arezzo. This time I come to find out why the Queen of Sheba fascinated the painter of the Madonna—Piero della Francesca.

There are two paintings by him that have to be seen by anyone seeking the true impact that the Queen of Sheba made upon the religious, artistic and cultural life of Italy: the procession of the Queen of Sheba and her entrance into Solomon's Temple.

The residents of Florence are commuting to work, pragmatic about the extraordinary civilisation cheek by jowl, as I stroll through the Piazza della Signoria, past the marble copy of Michelangelo's David, placed there in 1910.

The train station is a brilliant example of 1930s modernism, evoking the newfound confidence of the Italy of the time under its fascist leader Mussolini.

The train slips out of Florence, past smudged hills and Siena coloured houses, red earth and wheat fields, until, just less than an hour later, I am at Arezzo. There to meet me is Susanna; an art historian who has worked on the restoration of Piero della Francesca's celebrated frescoes. She has golden and dark-streaked hair and bright red lipstick and is wearing a black leather jacket and jeans. This is not going to be a conservative tutorial.

She knows I am looking for the Queen of Sheba, but first, she has another treat for me. We are going to see his Madonna. We head for the hills and she takes the corners with infectious enthusiasm, talking about the restoration of the frescoes and the moment, committed to memory, that she was THAT close to the Queen of Sheba's face.

First, we stop at the little village of Monterchi, home of the mother of Piero della Francesca. Women come here to drink from the springs, for there has been a belief since pagan times that they are a source of fertility. It is one of the excitements of Italy that some of the most stupendous art can be found in the

41

most unprepossessing locations. That is proved by the modest village museum in which we find the spectacular Madonna del Parto—and have it all to ourselves.

The wall on which it is painted was moved here from a local church. You can see here the method of the fresco—how he plotted his picture and transferred it to the wet plaster so that the colours were absorbed. In this picture, from 1459, the Madonna stands in the middle of a canopy of brocade. Angels on either side of her draw back the curtains. The symmetry is perfect. Piero Della Francesca adhered to Plato's teaching on the perfect geometric form of the universe and used his own version of a plumb line, a thread, a weight, and red pigment dots on the wall, to ensure dead straight lines.

He wrote the first essay on perspective. Isaac Newton was fascinated by the mathematical proportions of Solomon's Temple in the seventeenth century. Piero Della Francesca was grappling with the meaning of geometry a couple of centuries earlier.

He was clearly a master of colour. His father was a merchant who produced a plant to dye clothes indigo. Piero Della Francesca was brought up to respect beauty—and trade. The Madonna has a pure, impassive expression and is looking down, part of her own mystery rather than our lives. Her body however is real. She is visibly pregnant, and her hand is gesturing towards her belly. The orthodoxy of the Immaculate Conception was shaken by this defiant portrait of pregnancy. The figure has become a shrine for fertility.

There is a box in front of the fresco in which visitors have dropped notes to the Madonna. I pick one out. It is a plea to be given the gift of a child. Other women have written their hopes and fears for motherhood. Pregnant women are allowed free into the museum. The role of the mother is sacrosanct here. I find, to my surprise, that I am praying. I am a twenty-first-century rationalist, but the aura of compassion and mercy around the Madonna figure prevails here.

We drive on to Arezzo and park the car on the hill, close to a small statue of Petrarch, the great humanist, who was born here. One of his quotes is: "Rarely do great beauty and great virtue dwell together." Is the Queen of Sheba an example of that rarity or must we question her virtue?

According to the Abrahamic faiths, she was a pagan, foreign, impressed, converted. According to *The Kebra Nagast*, she was tricked, amorous and outwitting. She was instrumental in moving the Ark of the Covenant—the voice of God, from Israel to Ethiopia. It is in Ethiopia that her earthly, fecund, territorial qualities are realised. In Renaissance art, meanwhile, we see her as pure as frescoes.

We walk down the steep street to the plain-looking Basilica of St Francis. Inside, beauty and virtue co-exist in a manner that makes me laugh with delight. The bare room has its own little Sistine Chapel at the altar end, a divinely lit parlour of fresco colours. Piero della Francesca studied light and here is his mastery of it. The afternoon light floods through the long chapel windows, suffusing the frescoes. First, is the scene of the death of Adam, aged 900 (which cuts a bit of slack for the Queen of Sheba's extremely uncertain dates).

There are two groups in the foreground. On the right, Adam is sitting up, tended by an elderly Eve and his grandchildren. He has sent his son Seth to the angel Gabriel, shown in the background, to find the oil of salvation. On the left, Adam has died, and he is being given, instead of oil, a sapling that will form the holy tree of both good and evil. In the centre of the painting, behind the groups, is the great tree itself. When it was first painted it was in full leaf, but water damage and time have made it wintry. I hope we don't read too much symbolic significance into this.

The second scene, the best preserved and most beautifully symmetrical is that of the Queen of Sheba. Piero has tried a painting technique of tempera, which dries rapidly but allows deeper colours of blue. If done badly the blue can oxidise into the green. Here it works perfectly.

On the left-hand side, the Queen of Sheba falls in devout prayer before a log by a stream. Her ladies in waiting, graceful in dark red and green robes, Renaissance drapes, stand behind her in consternation. Behind, the grooms look after the horses, unconcerned by the vision. This is how Piero Della Francesca mixes allegory and realism. The Queen of Sheba herself is in profile, her hands raised in prayer.

The outlines are clear, her face is pale and her expression distant. Like Piero's Madonna, she exists in a different sphere. The landscape behind her is fresh—two trees in full leaf, the contours of hills, a clear Arezzo blue sky, with some white fleeces. The scene is separated from its sequel—the Queen of Sheba meeting Solomon—by a Corinthian column.

Solomon's palace looks Roman. The perspectives of architecture are pleasing. At the centre of the picture, the Queen of Sheba and her ladies in waiting, recognisable from the earlier scene, approach from the right. The Queen of Sheba is dressed in white, her head slightly bowed. Solomon is in a gold brocade cloak and a blue robe. Three fingers of one hand is tucked into his belt, which may be a gesture of appetite or of self-confidence.

He is resplendent; the Queen of Sheba is saint-like. She is drawn towards him, confiding in her terrible vision of the future of the cross. This is a portrait of dignity and melancholy. It is a wholly different scene from Veronese's hedonistic celebration of gifts. This was to have been a banquet of trade, but the Queen of Sheba has witnessed the arc of the Christian story, from the Creation to the death of Christ. She is a visionary. Her wisdom eclipses that of Solomon.

The rest of the frescoes continue the story. We discussed the role of the Queen of Sheba and the tree that was to become the cross when we looked at her religious significance. The legend of the true cross is the story of the tree by Abraham's grave that was cut down by Solomon and used as a bridge across a stream. The Queen of Sheba, on her way to Solomon, is about to cross the stream when she has a divine revelation that the wood will become the cross on which Jesus will be crucified.

Solomon orders that the wood from the bridge be buried. Three labourers carry the wood, with its marvellous detail of the wood grain. Their clothes are coarse, and the genitals of the front labourer are exposed in the effort. He is also carrying the wood as if it were the cross. He is a Flemish-style study in realism. He is also an allegory. The story is that three centuries after Christ's death, two Romans, Constantine and Maxentius, face each other in battle over who will rule the Roman Empire.

On the eve of the battle, Constantine is visited by an angel who shows him across. Constantine wins the battle and converts to Christianity with an edict in 313. His mother, Helen goes in search of the remains of the three crosses of Calvary. She is a different figure from the Queen of Sheba, dressed in black, more of a mother superior. The cross is then returned to Jerusalem. In the fresco, the shining city on the hill is recognisable as Arezzo.

Another three centuries, and in 615 AD, the King of Persia, Khosrow, invades Jerusalem and carries off the true cross to incorporate in his throne. The hubris is drawn by Francesca—the figure of Khosrow looks a little like the figure of God in the scene of the annunciation where the Virgin Mary learns her destiny. The battle scenes are a chance for Francesca to show off his banners—frankly, they are propaganda for the Crusades. The story ends when the Byzantine Emperor Heraclius defeats Khosrow in 628 AD bringing the true cross back to Jerusalem. An angel warns Heraclius against a triumphant entry. Instead, he carries the cross in the manner of Christ.

I was left thinking about the three women at the centre of the story. The Queen of Sheba, the Virgin Mary, and Helen. Bound by maternal destiny.

44

I walk back to the station. An hour later I am in Florence, walking along the Arno, looking for an al fresco supper in the remaining warmth of a late summer day. The paving stones are warm and worn from the sun and the tread of centuries of visitors. In this city, the past is always in the present.

My small story has been absorbed by millions of others. How many love affairs have taken place here? How many young mothers have stroked their stomachs in Florence—the womb of the Renaissance?

Life happens in chapters. My son is now grown up. He and his wife Anna live in Norfolk, near me and are trying to create a conservation paradise of the river, wildflower meadows and trees. Recently he bought his wife a dark green rowing boat and inscribed on it her name, Anna. They have a son.

Meanwhile, I married again have had two more children, followed many stories in life in journalism and have grown content and stout. The queen of Sheba's story is far from my life now, and yet I find her irresistible. In some sense, I feel that my story is bound up with hers because she is an expression of womanhood. Constantly recast, according to societal expectation, black, blonde, idealised, pure, dangerous, loving, vengeful, fleshy, symbolic. And somehow, despite all this, herself.

Chapter 4

Norfolk, Berlin, June The Secrets of the Queen of Sheba Lost in Time

I am now beginning my search in earnest, following desert paths that blow into sand storms. I am not the first person to develop a fascination for the Queen of Sheba. There was a once-famous British Arabist and adventurer called Harry St John Philby, father of the more famous Kim Philby.

The son was a double agent who was unmasked as a Russian spy in 1963 and lived for the rest of his life in Moscow. The father studied Oriental languages at Cambridge and converted to Islam in 1930.

He believed that he had found the land of Sheba, or Saba, in Marib in Yemen. There are inscriptions in masonry at Marib temple which suggest a Sabaean dynasty at around 500 BC and even earlier.

A brick tablet dated to the rule of Sargon King of Assyria takes us to 721 BC. Harry St John Philby presented his findings to the Royal Geographical Society in 1937 and was mortified to find his audience sceptical. Was she a chimera of history? Philby died in 1969, his book on the Queen of Sheba unfinished.

But he left important clues which I am following.

Harry St John Philby studied the characteristics of her Sabaean homeland: "An Arabian desert oasis, with rich palm-groves, orchards and cornfields on each side of a wadi: and all this being overwhelmed by one of the disastrous floods such as have, at rare intervals, been recorded through Arabian history."

"If, as seems likely, the tribe of Saba was originally (and in Solomon's time) in northern Arabia, its southwards thrust could possibly have occurred sometime between 650 and 500 BC. Thereafter it was well established in the southern home with which Arab tradition has always linked it."

In the centuries before the birth of Christ, the area that is now Yemen was developing great technological expertise in dams and irrigation. The archaeological evidence suggests the Arabs here were building advanced dams from the tenth century BC.

The Marib dam, one of the engineering marvels of the world, was in working order from the eighth century BC to the sixth century AD, when damage by the flood was repaired by Abraha, the Abyssinian viceroy, in AD 542.

There is no history of a southern Arabian queen but further north was a queen named Zabibe (of 'West-land', land of the Arabs) who was courteous, while another queen had to be subdued by military action. Who was this queen who did not know her place?

The inspirations could be wide for a troublesome Queen. My favourite spiritual descendant for the Queen of Sheba was Queen Zenobia, of Palmyra, Syria, who rebelled against Rome in 272 AD. She was, like the Queen of Sheba, interested in philosophy and open to different faiths. She reconciled Christians and Jews, although her own faith was derived from the pagan. Also, like the Queen of Sheba, she was a diplomat, presiding over a stable government and is a much-loved figure in Syria.

Her beauty was famous: in the Augustan History, a late Roman collection of essays, she is described as follows: "Her face was dark and of a swarthy hue, her eyes were black and powerful beyond the usual won't, her spirit divinely great, and her beauty incredible. So white were her teeth that many thought she had pearls in place of teeth."

Zenobia is certainly moulded from the same mythology as the Queen of Sheba.

Harry St John Philby point to inscriptions in the reign of the Assyrian King Sennacherib (705–681 BV) that tell us of three queens of the north, Yatie, Telhunu and Tabu'a. There are no mentions of any queen in Southern Arabia.

He writes: "The Queen of Sheba will have belonged to a far earlier and long-forgotten dispensation in which women undoubtedly played an important part in the affairs of the tribe. We have thus delved back as far as is ever likely to be possible in our search for the historical figure of the queen herself."

In the end, she defeated this indefatigable traveller and scholar.

There are emotional as well as historical reasons for us all wanting Saba to be in Yemen. This lovely civilisation has been devastated by civil war and its virtues forgotten. Architecture is one of Yemen's greatest achievements, mathematical sensibilities instinctual in its building of mud-brick tower houses.

The ancient town of Shibam, in Hadhramaut, calls itself the first city of skyscrapers. The tower houses, built from the soil, straw and water, Arabia date back to seventh and eighth centuries BC. They've survived the vicissitudes of age: sadly they are unable to withstand the bombardment of civil war.

There were other adventurers on her trail including the American Wendell Phillips, known as the American Lawrence of Arabia, the excavator in the 1950s of Myriam—the unforgettable alabaster face—which featured in the British Museum exhibition about the Queen of Sheba and which I keep in postcard form in front of me.

That is about as far as it got on the history of the Queen of Sheba. In my study in Norfolk, I look pensively out at the blue tits on the bird table and wonder if the riddle is beyond discovery. Harry St John Philby, Wendell Phillips. And then nothing.

But as I look through books of inscriptions and unpromisingly blurred photographs of granite, I come across the name of a German archaeologist, acknowledged as a leader in the field. She is called Iris Gerlach and she has been leading an expedition in northern Ethiopia to uncover a palace and temple.

I email Eyob Derillo and ask if he knows the site. Yes, he replies. It is called Yeha. It is probably the closest we will get to the Queen of Sheba.

Eyob says there is huge excitement in Ethiopia because the Yeha excavations are currently uncovering evidence in inscriptions on stone or bronze, dated to around the tenth century BC, of a kingdom called Saba or Sheba, a geographical forerunner of the Aksumite Kingdom.

Archaeologists now talk of a Sabaean culture from about 1,200 BC and recognisably Sabaean structures in Ethiopia in about 900 BC. We also have evidence of a monarchy named D'amat and Saba, which from its own royal inscriptions, held power in northern Tigray and Eritrea for some centuries from around 800 BC. The name Saba is usually associated with what is now Yemen.

But its use here raises questions about Saba and the African side of the Red Sea—indeed it gives colour to Ethiopia's claim that the Queen of Sheba came from there rather than from the Saba of Yemen.

My story turns to geography. I start spreading maps across my study desk in Norfolk like some old sea captain. I try not to get too caught up with modern national boundaries and to see the land and sea mass, a single territory embracing land on both sides of the Red Sea.

That gives me the Horn of Africa—Ethiopia, Somalia, Eritrea and Djibouti—and southern Arabia, now Saudi Arabia, Yemen and Oman. The Red Sea was crossed in the Axumite Kingdom, of Ethiopia, which briefly ruled Yemen, an empire that lasted from around 100 to 940 AD and is pretty well researched by historians. That's around 1,000 years after the period generally associated with the Queen of Sheba, but it demonstrates that, historically, the Red Sea was no impenetrable boundary. I notice that at one point the two lands are tantalisingly close, about twelve miles apart. Of course, boats must have crossed it. It still happens today, mostly fishermen, some pirates, a few terrorists.

This is the stretch of the Red Sea that absorbs me. I find the names of little archipelagos of the coast of Eritrea and worry about the danger for ships. I examine the shape of Socotra, the little island off the coast of Yemen, protected by a ring of rats. It is so hard to reach that its language, Zoroastrian religion and flora and fauna have remained ancient. This stretch of the Red Sea combines so much history, so many stories. It has always been a busy trading route, and with the exchange of goods and spices come to a brilliant cosmopolitanism. The Queen of Sheba was at the heart of this.

Egyptologists have given us other dates to play with. Between the thirtieth and twenty-fifth centuries BC, Egyptian ships sailed the Red Sea in search of myrrh. Then there were periods of disorder. The Egyptian empire collapsed after the death of Ramses III in 1167 BC.

The period attributed to Solomon and the Queen of Sheba was one of conflicting empires—Assyrian, Egyptian, Babylonian. Theban princes separated from Egypt and formed the kingdom that became Ethiopia. They went on to invade Egypt, establishing power from 722 to 663 BC. Then came the Assyrian invasions. The conquest of Egypt by Alexander Great was in 332 BC. In 30 BC, Egypt became a Roman province.

While there are no satisfactory historical records for the Queen of Sheba's appearance at a time that matches King Solomon in about 950 BC, there are secondary references and a scattering of clues. Modern techniques of genetic and metallurgy dating yield more information. The Bronze Age in this so-called Fertile Crescent region is becoming more vivid.

I am becoming convinced that this quest is all about the Red Sea. It was a hub of commerce, trading with merchants of India, Egypt and the Mediterranean. Those plucky little dhow trading boats, little more than reed bundles coated with mud, launched themselves into strong currents in order to trade.

I run my finger along with a picture of an antique map of the shoreline of southern Arabia. Here is a port in the east of Oman called Ras Al Jinz which was trading in the third on the millennium. Trade is as old as civilisation. The great modern port of Salalah is built on an older city of port of Al Baleed, which was a settlement in 2000 BC and by the fourteenth century was a favourite stopping place for Marco Polo. The history of trade and seafaring was founded in these Red Sea ports. I long to go to Salalah. I say the name out loud for its exotic sound.

There's a fascinating account of this region, written by an anonymous, Greek-speaking merchant in the first century AD. Of course, that is one millennium after the date attributed to the Queen of Sheba, but the Periplus of the Erythraean Sea (a periplus is a log listing ports and coastal landmarks, the sort of guide the skipper of a ship would use) tells us much about the region, including the Kingdom of Axum.

Axum's greatness was based on trade. Precious commodities, such as ivory, passed from the interior of Africa through Axum to the seaport of Edulis (now in Eritrea). Goods traded not only to the seaports of the Red Sea but also south into the mountains and east to join the incense trade and across the sea into Arabia.

I am content that the Kingdom of Axum stretched in time across the Red Sea, with territorial control over both sides. Axumite rulers conquered the Arab peninsula, including what is now Yemen, and called themselves Kings of Kush and Saba. The question is whether such a kingdom, spanning the Red Sea, was plausible 1,000 years before the development of the Axumite Empire.

The good news, in my search for the Queen of Sheba, is that there was in this region a tradition of female rulers. In the fifteenth century BC, the Egyptian Pharaoh Queen Hatshepsut launched an expedition to a distant country known as Punt or the Land of the God. Punt was above all a trading destination, rich in gold, ivory, and frankincense. Scholars have considered Sudan or Somalia, but many have settled on what is now Ethiopia or Eritrea.

We know there have been other female rulers in Ethiopia. The Acts of the Apostles, in the New Testament, refers to Queen Candace of Ethiopia and Kush (a region also covering modern-day Sudan) and explains: "Ethiopia even to this present day is ruled, according to ancestral custom, by a woman" (Acts 8.27). That ancestral custom is Ethiopia's strongest card for claiming the Queen of Sheba over Yemen.

The southern region of Meroe in Kush, on the Ethiopian side of the Red Sea, claimed ten queens between 260 BC and 320 AD. There is a legend of one queen pushing back Alexander the Great from his advance into Kush in 332 BC. And in a peace treaty between Rome and Meroe in 22 BC the Romans noted that the current queen of Meroe was a "very masculine sort of woman and blind in one eye."

The queens appear to have been fearsome military leaders as well as founders of dynasties. Al-Kahina was an eighth-century AD Berber warrior queen who sent her two sons into battle in order to start the first Arab dynasty. Among Arabs, a cult is recorded known as the 'Lady of Victory'. Aristocratic women would appear on the battlefield breasts exposed and hair loose, to spur the men into valour. Between the tenth century BC and the fifth century AD, Africa and Arabia were lands of queens.

The Egypt of the pharaohs fielded several regnant queens, including Hatshepsut and Cleopatra VII. In the course of 3,000 years, 7 Egyptian queens are counted. Twenty-one queens are recorded as sole regents in Ethiopia until the ninth century AD. Why were ancient times so much stronger on female rulers than the rest of history? And the legend of the queen of Sheba has eclipsed all other queens.

One of her eclipsing virtues is that Saba remained unconquered by foreigners until the fourth century AD. The dangers of the Red Sea and the desolate expanse of desert—the empty quarter, preserved it. Saba had its own language, although we know little of its administrative structure. We are unlikely to find out more just now on the Yemen side.

Archaeologists cannot go to Yemen at the moment. The structures they want to investigate are being damaged. The Marib dam itself, so important in our understanding of the ancient world, is believed to have been damaged in a Saudi airstrike in 2015.

I try to find a route to Aden.

The flights go from Cairo to Aden. They are packed full of NGOs and booked weeks ahead. I can get a flight out, but not a return one.

I look at other routes and times—Flights to Djibouti in the Horn of Africa are possible but again return flights are uncertain.

I try my friend General Ben Bathurst, retiring as head of the Cavalry. He has had a busy year—first as the ceremonial lead at the wedding of Prince Harry and Meghan Markle, then, in charge of the state visit of President Trump.

In preparation for the Queen's official birthday, Trooping the Colour, there is a smaller military ceremony called Beating the Retreat, at Horse Guards Parade, just behind Whitehall. It is soldiers, canon horses and musicians, plus fireworks. The spectacle, on a bright June evening, is of marching bands in formation while playing brass instruments, or pipes and drums. The regimental flag is lowered at sunset.

Ben Bathurst is in charge again. He invites the UK military ally the Omanis to take part and the Duchess of Cambridge to take the salute. We meet at a reception in Ben's quarters above the parade ground. Naturally, I mention the Queen of Sheba to the Oman delegation—the Chief of Staff of the Armed Forces and the Senior British loan service officer in Oman, Major General Richard Stanford—and they are enthusiastic.

Now I need practical help. I email Ben in desperation. Is there a way of getting into Yemen from Oman? He takes up my case with Major General Stanford. "There is a project that Sarah is doing on the Queen of Sheba. So if you could advise or put her in touch with Omanis that could help, that would be very much appreciated. However, we would like her back so please advise if you think it is a non-starter on security grounds."

The Major General is kindly but cautious.

Dear Sarah,

"It was good to meet you at Beating Retreat and to have a brief chat about the Queen of Sheba. My wife often recounts the tale of the Queen's hairy legs!"

For obvious reasons, I am not an expert at crossing the border from Oman to Yemen. I have been to both border crossing points and can report that there are extremely long queues. Getting out of Oman is, I am told, relatively easy, getting into Yemen is the hard bit. (This is because it is controlled by the Saudis.)

I know it is possible for Yemenis to move backwards and forwards with quite a lot of bureaucracy, but it can be done. However, I think it is much easier for those going to Mahra rather than further West to Marib since the Mahra tribe span the border.

As you will expect there will be a lot of people telling you it isn't safe to there. My view is that you could probably get there with the right connections and the tale of the Queen of Sheba will highlight the depth of culture in Yemen. I would love to be able to accompany you but that is probably a step too far for me! Try Lev Wood?

Yours ever,
Richard

As if happens, I do slightly know Lev Wood, the television explorer and also his agent Jo. We once spent a weekend together at the Tuscan palazzo home of my former newspaper boss Evgeni Lebedev. A feature of these weekends was all night dancing and drinking. By about 4:00 a.m., most guests, who included the British Prime Minister in waiting for Boris Johnson, were begging for mercy.

Lev was about to set off on an epic hike across the Caucasus mountain range between Russia and Iran. He needed to be in top shape. He alone, stayed the course with Evgeni Lebedev that night, matching him vodka to vodka until dawn. This man has a constitution to match his courage. I email Jo to ask how Lev got in and she says he did have a contact which he will pass on to me. I watch the Yemen episode of his travels on television. Finally, hear from a fixer in Cairo who thinks he can get me flights and a visa.

Days, weeks, months pass. No visa comes and hopes to start to fade. The security situation takes a turn for the worse. If I get to see Yemen, it will need to be from a boat in the Red Sea, in the manner of the Queen of Sheba.

What a kingdom it must have been. The well-irrigated gardens certainly sound like the land described by the Egyptian storyteller of the 1100s, Abu al-Hasan, 'Ali Ibn Hamzah al-Asadi—better known as Al-Kisa'I—who wove a romanticised setting for the childhood of the Queen of Sheba in the land of Kitor, within Saba. He talked of a beautiful city, shaded by palms and fed by canals, supported by a great dam.

The Queen, in his telling, is Bilqis, born of a liaison between a vizier of Kitor and a jinn—an Arab spirit—that had appeared before him in the form of a young woman. Bilqis was left in the desert, succoured by gazelles and raised by the jinns of the dunes, watched over by angels. Bilqis was to become the Queen of Sheba.

What has excited the attention of historians is not the jinns, but the dam. It has naturally been compared to the Marib dam in Yemen. One tribal tradition represents Bilqis as having built the dam and a palace for herself, another tradition claims that the dam was broken by this time and she repaired it. Some said the dam continued until the famous flood of al-Arim, in about 230 AD.

Germany is at the forefront of research into this region. And it is in Berlin that I come to find Iris Gerlach. I have tracked down her address and her photograph. And so on a tarmac melting summer day I am walking along the leafy academic quarter of Berlin to meet her.

Amid so much romantic fable, elements of historical fact and the slightly disputatious views of different archaeologists, it is time to take stock. I take the

Berlin overground across the city to meet Dr Iris Gerlach, of the German Archaeological Institute, another specialist in the region. I find the institute in a quiet road lined by foreign embassies, close to the city's Botanical Garden. With her pale, expressive eyes, auburn hair and clear skin, Ms Gerlach has a serene solidity about her. Generous with her time, she pushes me towards a logical, scientific course.

"Let's look at the facts, let's look at what we know."

She calmly lays out the boundaries for my expectations. "What we know is that in the second millennium, there was a history of movement of people from the north—from Palestine and Syria—to the south. Phoenicians. We have found pottery in Yemen."

"We see a culture change; there are the scripts, the southern Arabian monumental architecture, which suggest cities and palaces. We see the beginning of water distribution. We see complex kingdoms and controlled incense trade.

"There is evidence of caravan routes. There is clever politics with neighbours, a powerful expanding society, not through military conquering but through trade.

"The trade is in obsidian (a volcanic rock glass used for flint and knives). And at the end of the second millennium and the start of first millennium BC, there is contact between Saba and Tigray—you could travel by sailing boat."

My enthusiasm for my early research pours out. The Red Sea routes! From Sirwah to the Yemen port Al Hudaydah to Edulis harbour in Tigray—the northern Red Sea of Eritrea, Gulf of Zula. Which was part of the kingdom of Axum.

Dr Gerlach smiles and agrees. "Three thousand years ago, we know there was a civilisation in Edulis, there were strong winds further down so it makes sense to find a route from Al Hudaydah to Edulis." There were settlements along the way, and the centre was at Yeha. Here is a Sabaean temple, in limestone, recognisable in material and style to temples and housing in Yemen.

I walk down the road to the Botanical Garden and sit on the lawn in bright sunshine, writing up my notes. The trail is warm again. We know that women rulers were prominent in the ancient near east. Hatshepsut was the most famous, but there were at least two queens of Arabia in the eighth century BC—their names, Zabibe and Samsi, appear in Assyrian inscriptions. We know the importance of the spice trade during this period and that frankincense was transported by sea from Dhofar, in what is now Oman, up the Red Sea to Ezion

Geber, the biblical harbour close to what is now Eilat in Israel and Aqaba, over the border in Jordan.

We also know that the Sabaeans and southern Arabs were resourceful in their irrigation systems, and this expertise was employed in the Nile valley. We know the cereal grasses that were the basic foodstuff of the time along with grape, cumin and sesame. Teff, annual grass with edible seeds, is still widely grown in Ethiopia and imprints of it have been found in southern Arabian pottery. Flax was used for linen in southern Arabia as in Egypt. There is a constant resonance between Ethiopia, Southern Arabia and Egypt. The Queen of Sheba feels like a geographical composite.

My next hard question is that if she came from different places if she were a Red Sea queen, how can I find out what she looked like? The Queen of Sheba's beauty is so celebrated, that it must reveal something to me.

Chapter 5

London, Windsor, August A Wedding March Leads Me to the Royal Essence of the Queen of Sheba

It is the entrance of the Queen of Sheba which makes a greater impression than anything else. It is her arrival. I suddenly realise why I have such an emotional response to her entrance. It is Handel of course. His piece of music Entrance of the Queen of Sheba, in his oratorio Solomon, is a wedding march. It is how I entered a church in London, forty years ago, joyful, expectant. The marriage did not last, but the wedding was effervescent.

The fascination of the British monarchy with the Queen of Sheba can be traced to Handel. He spotted that she and Solomon represented an idealised form of monarchy and that he could bathe George I and George I in their glory.

I have glimpsed the nature of commerce in the time of the Queen of Sheba, through my conversation in Berlin with Iris Gerlach.

Handel lived in the eighteenth century as mercantile trading reached its greatest heights. What better time to stage the story of a trading queen who comes to admire a splendid monarch. Just as the British royal family now feels secure among the ranks of European monarchy, so were George I and II always happy to see a queen. The oratorio Solomon premiered in London in 1749. By a stroke of luck, the Royal Opera House is re-staging it and I have a ticket.

This piece of music brings the Queen of Sheba to life for me. I have been thinking about how she looks but this is how she sounds and feels. Music is my route to faith and for me, Handel is the Queen of Sheba.

Handel is a big-hearted composer and as he grew older he also became more religious. His sight started to falter and he found solace in the Church. He had already written his greatest work, Messiah, which secured him his place in history. As the Handel musicologist Jane Glover says to me when I meet fleetingly for coffee at the BBC.

"Messiah will be played at Lent, all over the world, for the rest of time."

He never married, and many have speculated over whether he was celibate or gay. Perhaps like Ruskin and Bede he was stirred by the Queen of Sheba, and composed in tribute to her music which will always conjure dazzling beauty and hope.

For me and many others, it stands for love, but in fact, Handel composed the entrance of the Queen of Sheba to depict statesmanship. She is, musically, a Queen. It may feel light, but it has majesty to it. And it is demanding of the soprano in its range of notes.

Glover is particularly interested that the Queen of Sheba has equal status in music. "It was written as a tribute to the king. There were the military pieces before, but then you have Solomon. It is a depiction of a stable monarchy. Handel was a friend of the monarchs, of George II and his wonderful wife Caroline, genuine friends. His funeral music for Caroline was genuine mourning for a friend."

Jane Glover's great specialisms are Handel and Mozart and there is one significant musical connection. Solomon and his Temple are the inspiration for the masonic brotherhood and there is a symbolic weight to Handel's music. Jane Glover has also conducted the Magic Flute—which is, in effect, a masonic opera. The Queen of the Night persuaded Prince Tamino to rescue her daughter Pamina from imprisonment by the high priest Sarastro. But Tamino is persuaded by the noble ideals of Sarastro's masonic community and joins it. Mozart was a mason, and the opera ends with an appeal to male order of reason, compared to the emotional excitement of the Queen of the Night. It is a journey from chaos to enlightenment.

In the final scene, Sarastro hails the sun's triumph over the night and dawn of wisdom and brotherhood. Jane Glover shakes her head: "You think it is going to be a frivolous pantomime and then it ends with a religious ceremony."

Clearly, I shall have to talk to the Masonic brotherhood, to grasp the woven legacy of Solomon and Sheba. But that is for another day.

At the Royal Opera House, Covent Garden on an unusually balmy Thursday evening I watch the fifty strong choirs on stage prepare to open Solomon, an oratorio performed infrequently these days. Behind them, giant mirror windows reflect the lights from the chandelier above. I am sitting next to a cellist called Tatty Theo, who waves at the second violinist in the orchestra pit. Tatty absolutely loves Handel. She thinks her husband, who runs London's Roundhouse arts venue, maybe looks a bit like him. And she is bouncing in her seat with excitement over the music. I ask if she thinks Handel, like Bach, might seem a bit churchy and austere for modern tastes. She looks at me with bottomless dark eyes and says: "Bach is from the head, Handel from the heart. He is so human."

Solomon is sung in alto, in the eighteenth-century tradition, by Lawrence Zazzo, who studied at Yale and Cambridge before the Royal College of Music. His job is to impress the Queen of Sheba with the splendours of his court. The role of the Queen of Sheba in Handel's Solomon is revealing. She is one of four women. The first is Solomon's devoted and virtuous wife. There are then the two harlots, brought before Handel to decide who the mother of the child is. One is defiant and reckless, accepting Solomon's instruction to cleave the child in two. The other sacrifices the child rather than see it murdered, and thus proves herself the rightful mother. This is the great judgement of Solomon.

Then there is the Queen of Sheba. In the original production, in March 1749, the Italian soprano Giulia Frasi sang the part of Solomon's queen, the first harlot, and the Queen of Sheba. English singers found Italian opera, which Handel had championed, too racy for their tastes. In this production, October 2018, Sophie Bevan plays the part of Solomon's Queen and of the first harlot. Susan Bickley plays second harlot and the Queen of Sheba. Susan Bickley has a stately serenity, a softly rounded face and short fair hair. She wears a pale grey shimmering dress beneath an embroidered darker grey coat.

The essential point about her relationship with Solomon is that it is not romantic. He loves his Egyptian wife. The Queen of Sheba is representing a great trading nation, not on the lookout for romance. Solomon lays on for his VIP guest some dazzling music. Handel approved of George II's patronage of the Arts, so this was quite a showpiece.

Also, in the audience at the Royal Opera House, that evening is Dr Ruth Smith, a Cambridge lecturer, who wrote Handel's Oratorio and eighteenth-century thought.

Dr Smith's interpretation of the historical context of the oratorio is that Britain is emerging from a long conflict, the War of the Austrian Succession, 1740–1749, which involved most of Europe in the Hapsburg Monarchy. You had also had King George II's War in America, and the Jacobite rising of 1745 in Scotland, in which 'Bonnie Prince Charlie' attempted to depose King George.

Handel set out to flatter King George by presenting an idealised view of monarchy, and a nation on the world stage. Britain is seen as a trading nation and a seafaring one. God is on the British side, just as he came to the rescue of the Israelites. When the Spanish Armada, sent to defeat Queen Elizabeth, was defeated by the British fleet in 1588, it was said that it was God who "blew with His winds and they were scattered." The idea of a 'Protestant wind' was popular in the time of George II.

Handel's Solomon shows a nation of peace and prosperity, which is what the British public longed for. The Queen of Sheba represents a great and admiring nation—in effect the rest of the world. A happy nation, as represented in the Psalms, is also a pastoral one. The language is of a verdant, rustic place—the sort of land recognisable from *Song of Songs*. The music is lyrical. Dr Smith likens the moods to the end of Shakespeare's Henry V. War leaves the land a neglected wilderness. Peace brings back fertile beauty.

Peace, prosperity, land cultivation and above all justice. Britain in the eighteenth century was proud of its constitution: a legal system above the crown. George II was a constitutional monarch, an ideal king who showed respect for the law. Thus the laws of the bible, as contained in the Ark of the Covenant, spoke to Handel's audience.

I drive home and listen to Sir Thomas Beecham's recording of the Arrival of the Queen of Sheba with the Royal Philharmonic Orchestra. Could we not have this as the National Anthem?

Solomon and Sheba is a celebration of visible wealth, but a reminder that wealth can be illusory and corrupting. After the Queen of Sheba, Solomon begins to believe that wealth and glory are his by right, so inviting the wrath of God, who granted him wisdom. What Handel understood about Solomon and Sheba was the importance of pomp and pageantry. George II asked him to compose the music for his coronation, for a pageant described by Jane Glover in her book:

The procession into the Abbey lasted over two hours. The king finally arrived in crimson velvet trimmed with ermine and gold lace. The Queen's dress was adorned with literally millions of pounds worth of precious stones. She carried a sceptre and an ivory rod complaining that the weight of her dress was "the worst thing I had to bear."

Later that week, I woke to an email from Ruth Smith, after I have written to thank her for her time:

Dear Sarah,

You are very welcome... I forgot to mention re Q of S in eighteenth-century England that her (biblical) words provide the text for the sermon at the coronation of George II, no less.

Go carefully as well as spicily, Ruth.

As soon as I can, I get to the archives and there it is, the Bishop of Oxford's Sermon Preach'd at the Coronation of King George II and Queen Caroline:

> In thefe words the Queen of Sheba addreffed King Solomon, having firft made a diligent and exact enquiry into the wife conduct both of his domelftick affairs and thofe of his kingdom. To the fame effect tho not fo full particular, are the following congratulatory exprefflions of King Hiram, to the fame Prince on his Accefflion to the Government: Becaufe the Lord hath loved his people, he hath made thee king over them

Later on the sermon underlines the theme:

> That wife and good Rulers are a fignal mark of the divine love and favour to any Nation: Becaufe thy God loved Ifrael, therefore made be thee king over them.

King Solomon. The Queen of Sheba. The House of Tudor. The House of Hanover. The House of Windsor. Across 3,000 years the divine right of kings continues.

Permission has come through for me and Eyob to visit the royal archives of Windsor, and on another balmy afternoon, we catch the train from Paddington. I buy sandwiches and water for us. I have struck up a comfortably maternal relationship with Eyob. Our journeys do not involve camels and treasure, but we are in search of wisdom, just as was the Queen of Sheba.

The essential point about the Queen of Sheba is that she was a monarch and in her own right. She did not rule as a consort. This is what makes her power so startling and suspected. In the Bible, her isolation is her strength. She admires Solomon but she does not submit to him. She leaves. For Ethiopians, her royal stamp is the course of their history—a direct line to Haile Selassie. In Britain too, there is a royal attachment to the Queen of Sheba. A great and powerful queen takes us inevitably to Elizabeth I. The Queen of Sheba was a great favourite of Queen Victoria. The notion of the harmonious universe, the basis for Solomon's Temple that was taken up by Pythagoras, is at the heart of the philosophy of Charles, The Prince of Wales. It is in the royal line here too.

Eyob has a friend at Windsor Castle called Emily Hannam who looks after the Near Eastern manuscripts. Chattering away about Handel we wander past the tourists coming to look at St George's Chapel—which has a renewed romantic interest since Prince Harry's marriage to Meghan Markle—and into the private rooms. None of us could imagine how that story would end.

The Queen of Sheba was a dark-skinned beauty who came to burnish the reputation of Solomon. In the Islamic tradition, she is a pagan who is converted by the power of Allah. But then isn't the Ethiopian version the most potent narrative? The Queen of Sheba submitted to Solomon but then went on to destroy him and his kingdom. Her son returned to steal away the Ark of the Covenant so that the light of God moved from Israel to Ethiopia. The modern psychodrama of Meghan and Harry has some of these elements. A stranger arrives who is either a force for good or destruction. As with, Queen Gudit, the story ends with the destruction of the temple.

The narrow, worn, red-carpeted corridor at Windsor leads to rooms that were once private chambers until Queen Charlotte, wife of King George III, pronounced them cold and damp and fled across the courtyard. The bibliographer Bridget Wright and Eyob have an earnest conversation about cataloguing while I look at the Elizabeth I stone fireplace with its heraldic carvings—including an emphatic crowned falcon representing Anne Boleyn. Elizabeth I minded about her legitimacy.

We move to the next room, to look at Elizabeth I's fine calligraphic handwriting, and Queen Victoria's annotated scribbles on the bestselling diaries of her holidays in Scotland.

There is greater drama to come. Emily, tall, dark-haired and bare-armed, wearing white gloves, strides over to some large, impressive looking books and reveals them to be false doors to inner shelves, from which she tenderly removes a seventy-folio illuminated book. It is the Persian Shah Nama of 1648, a gift in 1841 to Victoria. It was completed in May 1648 for Qarajaghay Khan, Governor of Mashhad, and presented to Queen Victoria by Kamran Shah, Sultan of Heart in 1839.

Bound in lacquered painted boards, it has a central floral arabesque design on a red background. The Shah Nama is the national epic of Iran and tells the history of Persia.

An inscription in the Windsor Shah Nama of 1648 explains why the gift counts: "The book of Shah Nama is the rhymed composition of the most eloquent of all poets, Firdausi. It compromises stories and annals of the wars of the kings of the eastern lands of Iran and the records of battles of the hero of the world, Rustam, son of Dastan—which has been cherished for many years—the servant (of God) the purest, the exalted, who has his place in the heavens, the most noble, the highest, Shah Kamran (is sending it) by way of a remembrance, a rare gift, and in the form of an offering, and remembrance for His Majesty (sic) whose exalted position is the seven heavens, the light of the pupil of magnificence, and sovereignty, the light of the garden of grandeur, and prosperity, the blossom of the flower garden of sovereignty, the first fruit of the orchard of superiority, the lightening of the rays of might (and) nobility, the flame which raises magnificence, Her Majesty, Queen of Sheba the King (sic) of England, who, during the siege, and after the siege, assistance and help were sent by the order of the one with exalted boundaries, the superior friend to this land, and those living there (this is) to be sent to the presence of the one with grace of custom."

This is how you pay a compliment.

Emily roots out Queen Victoria's journal entry on receipt of the book. She notes that it is clear before the Queen starts Persian or Hindu lessons because she muddles up the translation of the book's name.

> Sunday, 9 May 1841.
> Place of writing: (Principal Royal Residence) Buckingham Palace.
> After dinner, we looked at a very curious book sent to me by the wife of a Shah of Heart, called *The Book of Namah*, all in manuscript and splendidly illuminated.

The book is accompanied by a letter from the Foreign Secretary Lord Palmerston, sent from Carlton Terrace in 1841. Palmerston was in charge of British foreign policy at the height of imperial power.

The *Books of Kings* says Eyob, his face translucent with pleasure as he peers at the red green and gold decorated cover of the Shah Nama, as vivid and delicate in its design as a Persian rug.

We turn to the famous scene, spread across two pages, of Solomon and Sheba. He sits on a golden bed with the queen crossed legs beside him. She is wearing blue and gold with a matching cap. She has a moon-faced beauty, with almond eyes and joined eyebrows, an ideal of beauty of central Asia.

Significantly, she has her hand on his shoulder, a gesture of almost marital intimacy and companionship. It is not a ceremonial meeting of royalty, but a couple at ease with each other. Mind you, Solomon is not only markedly older in appearance, but he has a flamed shaped golden halo, so there is no doubt where divinity lies.

It is a scene of paradise. An angel fairy looks on from the left of the queen. On the right is a bird of paradise. There are elephants, deer, lions, a dragon, monkeys as well as peacocks and birds settled in branches of a tree. These are the birds and beasts controlled by Suleiman. The jinns are also there, the head jinn dressed below the waist in loose silk trousers, genie style.

It is a scene that can resonate with the British royal family. The divine right of kings has been a guiding notion. Furthermore, from Elizabeth I to Prince Charles, there has been a fascination with the mystical side of life. A key figure in Elizabeth I's reign was John Dee, an English mathematician, astronomer, astrologer and occult philosopher. He spent his later years trying to commune with angels, just as Isaac Newton later attempted to understand the mind of God through Solomon's Temple and the Ark of the Covenant. Science and magic are more closely connected than might be imagined.

Queen Victoria was enchanted by the Queen of Sheba. The Prince of Wales appears to be a disciple of Solomon. Prince Charles writes in his book *Harmony* about 'sacred geometry' found in temples, cathedrals and in nature. There are shades here of Solomon's 'natural wisdom'. Solomon's knowledge of the natural world is essential to his wisdom.

Prince Charles is fascinated, as was Isaac Newton, by Pythagoras, the Greek mathematician who is claimed to have travelled to Egypt in the sixth century BC to study with the priests. Pythagoras believed that numbers lay at the heart of beauty, for they explained the origins and nature of the world. According to the Italian writer and philosopher Umberto Eco: "Pythagoras marks the birth of an aesthetico-mathematical view of the universe; all things exist because they are ordered and they are ordered because they are the realisation of mathematical laws, which are at once a condition of existence and of Beauty."

Pythagoras's teaching, according to Prince Charles, is 'based upon the essential kingdom of all living things'. Geometry is what tames chaos. Prince Charles claims that Pythagoras saw the route to the Divine Mind was through numbers, the principles of proportion and harmony.

Prince Charles has attempted to re-enact this harmonic universe in his garden at Highgrove, in Gloucestershire.

At Windsor Castle, Emily moves to a computer in the wood-panelled library and finds more references to the queen of Sheba. Order of the Queen of Sheba (Ethiopia) Badge and Sash in case: Belonged to George V. Recipients of the purple and green sash with its crown and cross of triangles include Dwight Eisenhower.

Martini Innocenzo (1551–1623) Encounter between Solomon and Queen of Sheba in a colonnaded temple; many figures left and right, throne right with lion steps.

There is an engraving attributed by Bartsch to Marcantonio Raimondi after Raphael, with the warning that scholars have disputed the attribution and a photograph of a drawing which is very similar to that by Giovanni Francesco Penni now in The Louvre.

Then, fascinatingly, an engraving of the Queen of Sheba in profile looking a mix of Roman and Egyptian. Her hairstyle is angular and braided, and she has a long straight Roman nose and straight lips. She is wearing a robe flung over her shoulder and carrying a vase. The inscription reads: "And the Queen of Sheba saw the Wisdom of Solomon."

I have heard that there is one other very famous drawing here. It is by Holbein and it is of Solomon and Sheba. Emily hesitates; She thinks it may be downstairs. She could phone her colleague, but she is very busy. She does and by great fortune, her colleague is infected by our enthusiasm. Next thing, she is bounding up the stairs carrying in white gloves the drawing under glass.

There is Solomon looking down in a manspreading pose, a portrait of masculine satisfaction. There is a depth to the architecture, and he has lions engraved on his throne. He is unmistakeably Henry VIII. Holbein knows where his patronage lies. The Queen of Sheba, comely and rounded in the same form as she appears in Canterbury Cathedral's stained glass window, gestures up at him from below his thrown. Her entourage gathers in the foreground. They have brought great gifts. Not frankincense, but strawberries—bright red—and other bowls of delicacies. Eyob points out that while the Queen of Sheba looks as British as Solomon, some of her courts have flatter noses, which suggest some recognition of African appearance.

There are other splashes of colour in the drawing. Both Solomon and the Queen of Sheba are wearing gold crowns. The backdrop is a rich blue with gold stars, almost fleur de lis. There is one other curious photograph in the collection. It is of Queen Victoria's Tableaux Vivants—a fancy dress portrait of the court of Solomon and Sheba featuring members of the royal family.

Queen Victoria's fascination with the Ethiopian version of events is borne out by her attachment to the sons of the country. In Saint George's Chapel, there is a curious plaque, below an Ethiopian cross.

Near this spot lies buried Alemayehu, the son of Theodore, King of Abyssinia. Born 23 April 1861. Died 14 December 1879. This tablet is placed here in his memory by Queen Victoria. I was a stranger and ye take me in.

Here is a strange Victorian tale. Prince Alemayehu of Ethiopia was the son of Emperor Theodore of Ethiopia. He was taken to Britain when he was seven years old along with many national treasures, after his father, a national hero, killed himself with a gun given to him by Queen Victoria.

There is a photograph of the young boy taken during the 1868 British Napier expedition, which set out to rescue some European prisoners. His father the emperor held the Europeans captive because his letters to Queen Victoria went unanswered. Sir Robert Napier came with thousands of soldiers and followers and the emperor released the prisoners before killing himself.

Alemayehu became a ward of Queen Victoria, having been introduced by Captain Tristram Speedy, an explorer who adopted native Ethiopian costume and is seen as the inspiration for a character in one of Rudyard Kipling's short stories. He took care of the boy—sleeping in the same bed, which causes modern consternation—at his home near Osborne House—a holiday retreat of Victoria—on the Isle of Wight. Queen Victoria doted on the young African, describing him in her diary as "a pretty, polite, graceful boy."

But she conceded that "his was no happy life, full of difficulties of every kind."

There is a photograph of him in his uniform at Rugby School—the setting for Tom Brown's Schooldays—looking wistful. He went on to Sandhurst, the British military academy where army officers are trained, and died aged 18 of pleurisy. Queen Victoria believed he had led a sad life, far from home. The Ethiopian Government has requested the return of the prince's body, but it is an awkward matter. He is buried in the catacombs, and there is alarm about digging up royal graves. I ask Eyob what he thinks. He sighs that it is not easy.

It has been a great pleasure getting to know Eyob. In a country where most users of social media are posting angry comments about political division, I look forward to his tweets about illuminated manuscripts. I watch him bent respectfully over one of Windsor's Ethiopian parchment books. He smells it and touches it lightly. Rubbed with frankincense.

Of course, it is impossible to think of the Queen of Sheba without contemplating Elizabeth I. Two and a half thousand years before the British queen, The Queen of Sheba sits at the top of a maritime power that believes above all in trade. Elizabeth I would have appreciated her knowledge of spices. Elizabeth's was the great age of English exploration and the foundation of the British Empire. English merchants went in search of Oriental spices, particularly cinnamon, peppers and cloves. Sea routes were established so that they could trade with India and the East Indies.

In a scenario not unfamiliar today, most trades were with Europe, but the English wanted to trade with the rest of the world. Elizabeth I handed out a patent to the Levant company to bring back grapes, wine and silk. The greatest trading company was the East India Company, created in 1600 to challenge Spanish and Portuguese control of the spice trade. It faced tough competition from the Dutch East India Company, which became the wealthiest commercial operation in the world in the seventeenth century with 200 ships. So great was demand that, during the seventeenth and eighteenth centuries, spices traded on margins of 400 per cent per voyage.

The names of Christopher Columbus, the fifteenth-century Italian explorer who sailed to the Americas on behalf of Spanish monarchs, and his contemporary, Vasco da Gama, the Portuguese explorer who voyaged to India, had earlier been made famous by returning hoards of treasure spices. Columbus boasted a deeper purpose for his explorations, including an intention to finance a crusade to save the Holy Sepulchre of Jerusalem from Muslim control, but trade rather than faith was imperative.

By the seventeenth century, the English and the Dutch entered the spice race propelled by 'the Protestant winds'. In 1601—three years before the death of Elizabeth I—a fleet left England under the name of the Company of Merchants of London trading into the East Indies. Vessels had names such as Clove and Peppercorn. It was the beginning of the great trading area.

King Solomon. The Queen of Sheba. The House of Tudor. The House of Hanover. The House of Windsor. Trade, marriage and monarchy. Across 3,000 years the divine right of kings continues.

I must trace the royal journey back to its source. I am getting to know the Queen of Sheba but I cannot isolate her from King Solomon. In order to understand her, I must understand him. What was the wisdom of Solomon? And what were the secrets of his temple?

Chapter 6
London, October The Magic and Mystery of Solomon

Where were you when I laid the earth's foundations? The Queen of Sheba travelled to see Solomon and to witness his wisdom and glory. In Handel's oratorio Solomon, she is there to validate him. He may have unfairly eclipsed her, but Solomon and his Temple are at the centre of her story.

In order to get closer to her, I must find Solomon.

The scholar Israel Finkelstein co-wrote the seminal book *David and Solomon* with Neil Asher Silberman. It opens: "From the soaring cathedrals and elegant palaces of medieval Europe to the hushed galleries of world-famous art museums to America's backwoods pulpits and Hollywood epics, the story of ancient Israel's kings, David and Solomon, is one of the western civilisations most enduring legacies.

"The figures of David—shepherd, warrior, and divinely protected king—and of his son Solomon—great builder, wise judge, and serene ruler of a vast empire—have come timeless models of righteous leadership under God's sanction. They have shaped western images of kingship and served as models of royal piety, messianic expectation and national destiny."

Eyob tells me to look beyond the kingship: the magic matters and Solomon's magic takes us to the secret of the universe.

Not far from the British Library is another building, which houses the collection of the Welcome Trust, the scientific—and it turns out the occult collection of work which has formed human knowledge.

It is raining hard and I shake off my umbrella by the desk. I have come to look at a book called *The Key of Solomon*. It is not on display. It may be too potent and dangerous for that. The occult can be used for good or for bad. Solomon is revered in the Abrahamic faiths, but he also has admirers on the wilder shores of religion. In the Middle Ages, the occult was a branch of science, now it has acquired a different meaning.

The seventeenth-/eighteenth-century physicist and mathematician Isaac Newton was the Age of Discovery hero, celebrated for his ground-breaking work on gravity, motion and other science. But he also conducted parallel investigations into the occult, biblical history and took a particular interest in the temple of Solomon. He revered the king of Israel as a figure of ancient wisdom who passed down hidden knowledge.

The economist Maynard Keynes, who made a study of Newton's reconstruction of the floor plan of the Temple of Solomon and masses of accompanying calculations and theories, wrote that Newton saw "the whole universe and all that is in it as a riddle, as a secret which could be read by applying pure thought to certain evidence, certain mystic clues which God had hid about the world to allow a sort of philosopher's treasure hunt to the esoteric brotherhood."

For the scientists, philosophers, alchemists and scholars of the Middle Ages, the Renaissance and even into the Age of Discovery, for the Knights Templar who mounted the Crusades against Islam, for occultists of the nineteenth century, Solomon was a significant, indeed crucial figure.

He was studied by the Elizabethan court astronomer John Dee, who also drew heavily on Egyptology. In modern times, these interests have tended towards dark practices of black magic—arcane, sinister material understood only by the 'chosen'.

The origins of the belief that there is a key to all knowledge are derived from Solomon having received from God the gift of wisdom—the wisdom he was prepared later to share with the Queen of Sheba. The myth goes that Solomon wrote down all his knowledge for his son Rehoboam—half-brother of Menelik, by another wife. Rehoboam buried the script in an ivory casket in his tomb. The legend was enhanced by Josephus, the first century AD Jewish historian, who claimed that Solomon wrote 3,000 books containing exorcisms and incantations.

The *Testament of Solomon*, written in Greek sometime in the first five centuries AD concerns the building of the Temple. This is the story of the angel Michael presenting Solomon with a magic ring, and of how the Seal of Solomon could control demons. Solomon's Temple is constructed by magic.

For example at one point, Solomon is vexed by the keystone, which is too heavy. He sends a servant to Arabia with a leather flask and seal and tells him to capture the demon wind in the bottle and to secure the flask with his seal. The following day King Solomon enters the half-built temple and sits in dismay thinking about the heavy stone. Then the flask stands up, walks around some seven steps and pays homage to Solomon.

The demon Ephippass has retained its power within the bottle but is commanded by Solomon. The demon is ordered by Solomon to lift the keystone, which he does, on a pillar of air. The construction of Solomon's Temple was seen by the believers who followed both as a superb achievement of masonry and an act of mysticism. Sir Isaac Newton believed the measurements of the temple, and particularly its inner sanctuary, the Holy of Holies, in which was kept the Ark of the Covenant, would reveal to him the mind of God.

Was this what the Queen of Sheba learned from her hard questions of Solomon and is this why she encouraged Menelik to bring back the Ark of the Covenant from Solomon's Temple to Ethiopia?

Solomon had other gifts—he could command the birds and the beasts. He was a master of nature. The hoopoe bird which bore a message to the Queen of Sheba came from Solomon.

The Temple of Solomon is believed to bestow mystical powers, which are woven into an oral tradition and have been richly illustrated by artists. The flying carpet of Solomon, carrying the king by the winds, and accompanied by birds, is a theme in Arabian storytelling. The designs may include the four rivers of Paradise or the Tree of Life.

The fabled carpets became increasingly detailed and magnificent. The Persian Emperor Khosrow commissioned a carpet to celebrate his conquest of Yemen in AD 562. It featured a garden in which the earth was gold, the water crystal and the flower beds full of gems. In *The Book of Omens*, a book of texts and illustrations on the art of divination that was created in Iran and Ottoman Turkey in the sixteenth and seventeenth centuries, we see a compelling illustration of Solomon and the Queen cross-legged on a divan. A jinn angel, of Arabian appearance, and with blue wings, stands to watch over the Queen, black-haired and pale-skinned, who leans towards her.

Solomon addresses his vizier on the other side, and a demon beneath, with eyes of fire, looks on. There is a tree of life and above it, strange and brightly coloured birds fill the sky. Below the divan, the garden is also filled with creatures, wild animals, horses, griffins, rabbits—some animals real, some imaginary. The Queen, like Solomon, has a halo-like headdress of flame.

I begin to wonder something about the Queen of Sheba. The knowledge she gained from Solomon could be used for good or for ill. Was the removal of the

Ark of the Covenant an act of consent or one of betrayal? It certainly led to the ruin of Solomon.

I look again at the passages from *The Kebra Nagast.*

"And it came to pass that after these things she became with child by him and she said unto him: 'I am going to return to my country and to my kingdom and what shall I do with thy child it if be that God shall desire to give him life?'"

He gives her a ring: "Guard carefully this ring and covenant with me that thou wilt not in the smallest degree break the conditions of the true and righteous covenant that existeth between us and God, the Governor of the Universe, the God of Abraham, and Isaac and Jacob the God of my father David, shall be the witness between and between thee. And when thou does send my son to me, give him my ring, and let him wear in on his own hand and I shall know that in the very truth he is your son and I will make him king and send him back to thee."

The son of Solomon and Sheba, called Menelek, does indeed return, but it is to take the sacred Ark of the Covenant from Solomon's Temple and deliver it to his mother in Ethiopia. With this gesture, according to Ethiopian beliefs, he brings about the ruin of Israel, as well as of his father.

"That same night Solomon saw a dream in which the sun came down from heaven, and shone brilliantly over Israel, and then departed to Ethiopia to shine there forever. Then a sun more brilliant came down sand shone over Israel and the Israelites rejected the Sun and destroyed it and buried it but that Sun rose again and ascended into heaven and paid no further heed to Israel. Solomon troubled that the departure of the Sun from Israel typified the departure of God."

And the great Solomon, on whom Jerusalem's hopes had rested, was diminished from then on. The loss of the sacred Tabernacle caused his love of God to wane, and he devoted himself to women for the past eleven years of his life. He married Makshara, an Egyptian princess who seduced his household into worshipping her idols, then implored her husband until he carried out an act of worship at an Egyptian temple.

Solomon was aged 60 when he died. He was rebuked by the angel of death for his weakness towards women, his hubris and his dedication to wealth for his own ends rather than for the glory of God.

In other words, the Queen of Sheba had the final word. Solomon won the battle of wits, but she won the war. She had come in search of wisdom, and Solomon gave her all she desired.

She admired Solomon, but did she feel he was worthy of divine wisdom? Perhaps she simply recognised divine wisdom and thus became the rightful recipient of God's favour. God's gift to Solomon was wisdom, but it eventually became flawed by hubris. The Queen of Sheba was less grandiose in her claims. She took counsel from her advisors and ruled justly. As a role model of leadership, I would say that she outclasses Solomon.

The diminished power of Solomon after her departure and the subsequent rise of Ethiopia may explain something that has puzzled me about the Queen of Sheba. Why does a great Queen and stateswoman suffer such catastrophic public relations in folklore telling of her story?

There is the deformed foot that she acquires in some versions. Worse, she becomes merged with the devilish folk figure of Lilith, who steals babies from their cots and strangles them.

Solomon has magic powers and she acquires them and perhaps uses them against him. But, according to *The Kebra Nagast*, he used trickery to seduce her in the first place.

This is how the affair happened in full: "Solomon longed for her greatly and entreated her to yield to him. But she would not surrender herself to him, and she said unto him: 'I came to thee a maiden, a virgin; shall I go back despoiled of my virginity and suffer disgrace in my kingdom?'

"And Solomon said to her: 'I will only take thee to myself in lawful marriage—I am the King and thou shalt be Queen'. And she never answered him a word."

And he said unto her: "Strike a covenant with me that I am only to take thee to the wife of thine own free will—this shall be the condition between us; when thou shalt come to me by night as I am lying on the cushions of my bed, thou shall become my wife by the Law of Kings."

She does not come, and so he orders a spicy banquet and for her to be given only sips of water. If she asks for water, servants are instructed to reply: "Thou wilt find no water except by the couch of the king."

Almost dying of thirst, she eventually seeks water from the king. She then submits to their covenant: "And she gave herself into his embrace willingly and yielded to his desire, according to that which she had covenanted him."

If you read Song of Solomon, what happened between King Solomon and the Queen of Sheba was an honest and open exchange of passions. In *The Kebra Nagast*, the affair was conducted through riddles and illusion. A glass floor that looks like a pond, a banquet with a secret ingredient. Nothing is as it appears.

Solomon is aided in the building of his temple by spirits, and the Queen of Sheba, who is a pagan sun-worshipping queen, is part jinn or spirit herself. It is a relationship of the occult.

I write down the word in my notebook just as the keeper of the books at the Welcome collection takes a book from the shelves and then hands it to me: it is an occult manuscript once sought by the entire world, a work that promises to distil all human knowledge. It is a single volume under plain green cover: *The Key of Solomon the King*. Feeling a little nervous lest I unleash some kind of supernatural power, I turn the pages to an important chapter: Of the Experiment of Seeking Favour and Love.

The instructions are intricate: "If thou wishest to perform the Experiment of seeking favour and love, observe in what manner the Experiment is to be carried out, and if it be dependent upon the day and the hour, perform it in the day and the hour required, as thou wilt find it in the chapter concerning the hours; and if the experiment be one that requireth writing, thou shalt write as it is said in the chapter concerning the same; and if it be with penal bond, pacts, and fumigations, then thou shalt cense with a fit perfume as is said in the chapter concerning suffimigations; and if it be necessary to sprinkle it with water and hyssop, then let it be as in the chapter concerning the same; similarly if such experiment require characters, names, or the like, let such names be written as the chapter concerning the writing of characters, and place the same in a clean place as hath been said. Then thou shalt repeat over it the following Oration:

"O Adonai, Most Holy, Most Righteous and most Mighty God, Who hast made all things through Thy Mercy and Righteousness wherewith Thou art filled, grant unto us that we may be found worthy that this experiment may be found consecrated and perfect so that the Light may issue from Thy Most Holy Seat, O Adonai, which may obtain favour and love. Amen.

"This being said, thou shalt place it in clean silk, and bury it for a day and a night at the junction of four cross-roads; and whensoever thou wishest to obtain any grace or favour from any, take it, having first properly consecrated it according to the rule, and place it in thy right hand, and seek thou what thou wilt it shall not be denied thee. But if thou doest not the Experiment carefully and rightly, assuredly thou shalt not succeed in any manner.

"For obtaining grace and love, write down the following words: Sator, Arepo, Tenet, Opera, Rotas, Iah, Iah, Iah, Enam, Iah, Iah, Iah, Kether, Chokmah, Binah, Gedulah, Geburah, Tiphereth, Netzach, Hod, Yesod, Malkuth, Abraham, Isaac, Jacob, Shadrach, Meshach, Abednego, be ye all present in my aid and for whatever I shall desire to obtain. Which words being properly written as above, thou shalt also find thy desire brought to pass."

Did Solomon practice this spell on the Queen of Sheba? Was this the secret behind his amorous successes, his 700 wives and 300 concubines? Many were prepared to think so.

The copy of the work I am looking at is in the collection of the Welcome Trust, the philanthropic organisation built on a fortune built on pharmaceuticals. The early twentieth-century pharmaceutical mogul and philanthropist Henry Welcome collected nineteenth-century works of the occult. The book, translated by the occultist Liddell Macgregor Mathers from Latin manuscripts held at the British Museum, was published in 1889.

Ross, the mild-mannered Scottish librarian, seems a little sceptical about the contents. The urtext said in legend to have been created by Solomon himself, is believed by many to be a lost manuscript. Ross shrugs that he does not believe it ever existed.

This passage from Job sets out the harmony and order of God's design for the earth as if it were Solomon's Temple:

> "Where were you when I laid the earth's foundations?
> Speak if you have understanding.
> Do you know who fixed its dimensions
> Or who measured it with a line?
> Onto what were its bases sunk?
> Who set its cornerstone
> When the morning stars sang together
> And all the divine beings shouted for joy?"
> (Job 38:4–7)

Kabbalah, the strain of Judaism which has created its own philosophy, also looks to Solomon's Temple for the secrets of the knowledge of the universe. The Kabbalistic teacher Z'ev ben Shimon Halevi states that the construction of the Temple and the seven-branched candlestick—whose design was given to Moses on Mount Sinai, were formed from the Tree of Life, a symbol of creation.

The physical diagram of the Tree built into the Temple was lost when this first Temple was destroyed by the Babylonians. As for King Solomon, he is regarded by Kabbalah as one of the great saints and sages along with Moses, Buddha and Jesus.

More than 2,000 years after the king and his construction, Solomon and the temple was the inspiration for the Knights Templar, the Crusaders of Christian Europe that fought Muslim forces across the Holy Land. Three thousand years later, Solomon and the temple continue to influence the freemasons, the secretive society whose members pledge reciprocal support and use arcane symbols, rituals, and handshakes. The groups are connected, possibly because the Templars taught stonemasons building techniques and geometry, which were to become part of the tradition of freemasonry.

The Knights Templar—the Poor Fellow Soldiers of Christ and of the Temple of Solomon also known as the Order of Solomon's Temple—were founded in 1119, twenty years after Jerusalem had fallen to a Christian siege at the end of the First Crusade. The order was founded on principles of chastity, obedience and poverty. Its role, at first, was to protect the influx of western pilgrims travelling to a Holy Land recently restored to Christian control. Their symbol was of two armed brothers sharing a single horse. The order grew rich and influential as it spread through Europe.

For the Knights Templar, defence of the 'eternal city' Jerusalem was core. The prophet Ezekiel said that God set Jerusalem 'in the midst of nations'. In the Europe of the twelfth century, the city was the centre of the cosmos, said to be the place where the heavens were manifest.

Its headquarters were where the al-Aqsa mosque now stands on Temple Mount in Jerusalem—then as now one of the most congested areas of land in the world. For Jews and Christians, this was the site of the first temple of King Solomon. For Muslims, this was the Noble Sanctuary, the place where Muhammad ascended into heaven.

The spiritual guide for the Templars was Bernard of Clairvaux, a French abbot and the founder of the Cistercian order. Cistercians believed in a simple, ascetic existence and hard work. The Templars wore habits of white, as did the Cistercians, signifying purity and chastity. The red cross was added in 1139. The company of women was banned: "A dangerous thing, for by it the old devil has led men from the straight path to paradise... the Knighthood of Christ should avoid at all costs the embraces of women, by which men have perished many times." By the late 1140s, the Templars were known across the Christian world.

Over the next 200 years—amid the defeats and victories of successive crusades—the power, wealth and influence of the Knights Templar across all of Christendom increased. They were regarded with some suspicion, as a society with its own arcane rituals and membership rules. In 1307, King Philip IV of

France, in financial debt to the order, imprisoned, tortured and burned at the stake a group of prominent members. In 1312, Pope Clement V ordered the society to be disbanded.

Given this chequered history of courage, chivalry, mythology and skulduggery, I am excited to be invited to meet the current Grand Secretary of the Knights Templar in Britain. On the way, I look in at the blockbuster exhibition at the Tate Gallery of the Pre-Raphaelite painter Edward Burne Jones. Burne-Jones used Arthurian and Renaissance myths to create a world of dream-like beauty. The exhibition features his celestial stained glass window designs. The paintings are of knights, maidens, pilgrims, places of enchantment. The Queen of Sheba was the precursor to all this. She is the mother of legends.

Their headquarters of the Knights Templar are in a gracious building in St James's Street, close to Clarence House, home of the Prince of Wales, and most of the capital's traditional, rather stuffy gentlemen's clubs. This is the traditional heart of London. The surrounding shops sell cigars, hats, vintage wine, country and shooting wear. I sweep up the steps of Mark Masons' Hall, which smells of past Sunday roasts. In the hallway is a large portrait of Prince Michael of Kent opposite a slab of limestone on a podium. The inscription reads: 'Stone from King Solomon's Quarries—Jerusalem'.

The block was cut in 1939 from a site chosen by the then grand master of the freemasons, from the royal quarries of Solomon, beneath the temples of Jerusalem. The stone is a hard crystalline limestone that, when dressed, reveals many traces of seashells and fossils. It takes an excellent polish and the general effect might well have inspired Josephus to describe the Holy Temple as 'glistening in the sun like a mound of snow'.

A compact, sturdy Welshman extends his hand. This is Ryan Williams, the Grand Secretary of the Knight Templars. He takes me to his office at the top of the building and describes the job. He says that, frankly, it is has become harder since the publication of Dan Brown's Da Vinci Code because the first question that Knights Templars get asked is: where is the Holy Grail?

Mr Williams, a former banker now in his 50s, has to explain that the Templars have ceremonial links to the original Knights Templar, but he is no Richard the Lionheart. "Different periods," he says, sensibly. "They go back to twelfth and thirteenth centuries, modern-day Knights Templar go back to the eighteenth century."

However, his ceremonial dress—he has a meeting of the Great Priory the next day when he will be kitted out—is familiar; a tunic with a giant cross on it, with a cape-like mantle over it. The Knights Templar still wear belts and swords. The emblem is still two knights upon one horse, a symbol of brotherhood. The initiation ceremony welcomes you as a Jerusalem pilgrim. And, unlike other Masonic orders, you have to proclaim a Christian belief to join the Knight Templars.

The story of Solomon's Temple runs through the orders. Some refer to lost words hidden in inscriptions on a marble pedestal, within a secret vault. One order focuses on the death of Solomon and his final instruction to his heir on the art of statesmanship. A more practical sounding order is Mark Degree, which has strong traditions of construction of Solomon's Temple.

In Mark Degree, you wear an apron rather than a robe. The emblem is of a plumb line with an axe going through it, within a circle of hyssop leaves. The plumb line is the instrument used by builders to keep straight lines. The axe signifies the role of the junior warden to cut off the hands of those trying to steal wages. These Masons are both upright and stern.

There are two branches of male societies which can be traced to Solomon. There are the Knight Templars and then there are the Freemasons or 'sacred builders'.

I have with me the splendidly named *General History, Cyclopedia and Dictionary of Freemasonry*, by Robert Macoy. Its subtitle alone feels worth a separate book: 'Containing an Elaborate Account of the Rise and Progress of Freemasonry, and Its Kindred Associations Ancient and Modern'. The cyclopaedia has many Solomonic references. An abaciscus is the square mosaics supposedly used on the floor of Solomon's Temple. An abditorum—in archaeology a secret place where documents can be concealed—is said to have been in the two columns at the entrance of Solomon's Temple.

This book emphasises the lineage of Solomon and his Temple. It pays tribute to the Egyptians and their priests who "secured the mysteries of their religion from the knowledge of the vulgar or uninitiated by symbols and hieroglyphics, comprehensible alone to those of the order." The fraternity of ancient Egypt was known as the Sacred Builders, the masons who understood the mysteries of the pyramids and their construction.

The Israelites took this knowledge with them to the 'promised land'. When his father King David instructed Solomon to build the temple, he sought advice from the Hiram, King of Tyre (in Phoenicia, which is now part of Lebanon and Syria). The King of Tyre sent him cedar timber, and a mason, who took the title of Deputy Grand Master or Principal Surveyor and Master of the Work.

Solomon is said to have employed enlightened and religious men who understand geometry and proportion to oversee the work. The General History records: "This arrangement produced the happiest effects, and introduced among the fraternity that perfect harmony and universal brotherhood."

The accuracy of the mathematical construction and system of distribution had a practical effect. Solomon's Temple took seven years to build. St Peter's Cathedral in Rome, 150 years, St Paul's in London thirty-five years. The splendour of Solomon's Temple was destroyed 400 years after it was built. In 588 BC, Nebuchadnezzar of Babylon ransacked Jerusalem, set fire to the Temple, and took thousands of captives. In 536 BC, Cyrus, the King of Persia, liberated Jerusalem from Nebuchadnezzar and called for another Temple.

The history and power of the masons throughout Europe developed over hundreds of years as they formed societies, sometimes to the suspicion of rulers and Popes. They've been the subject of Papal Bulls, banned by governments, allowed to meet again. Today freemasonry flourishes in America, Europe and the United Kingdom. What are they up to? How much power do they have? And what is the role of Solomon?

After several months, I get a date to visit Freemasons Hall, in Great Queen Street an impressive building on the edge of Covent Garden, in the middle of London. Dr David Staples, a former hospital consultant, greets me. This is the United Grand Lodge of England—a Masonic meeting place since 1775. It's a grand, white stone building that houses both Masonic chambers and a library. In recent years, it has been supplementing funds by hosting catwalk shows in London Fashion Week and hiring out space for glamorous parties. Who would have expected to find the Vogue editor Anna Wintour holding court in a masonic lodge?

Former Masons commemorated here include Field Marshal Kitchener (1850–1916) Secretary of State for War in 1914, Field Marshal Douglas Haig (1861–1928) Commander of Chief of the British Army on the Western Front from 1915, and a member of the Grand Lodge of Scotland.

So were the American heroes General MacArthur, General Patton and Franklin Roosevelt. There is a life-size portrait of George Washington hanging on the wall, one of the many US Presidents from the order. The freemason symbol of the Eye of Providence is still on dollar notes. It symbolises the watchfulness of God—accountability being a first principle of the freemasons.

The great catch, so far as London is concerned, is Sir Christopher Wren, the architect of St Paul's. Scholars have argued over the evidence of his membership, but a Freemason's lecture in 2011 made a persuasive case. It matters because Freemason's trace their inspiration to those who built Solomon's Temple, so you would like some architects on the books. Sir Christopher Wren was also a champion of science. He held professorships in astronomy in both London and Oxford and made significant contributions to the fields of mathematics, microscopy and anatomy. The fascinating thread through the story of Solomon and Sheba is that they encompass science as well as religion. It is an understanding of both that begins to shed light on the knowledge. Or to put it another way, knowledge is light.

The building of the Temple is described in terms a freemason would immediately recognise. Its measurements are precise, its purpose clear:

1 Kings: 6.

And the house which King Solomon built for the Lord, the length thereof was threescore cubits, and the breadth thereof twenty cubits and the height thereof thirty cubits.

And the porch before the temple of the house, twenty cubits was the length thereof, according to the breadth of the house; and ten cubits was the breadth thereof before the house.

And for the house he made windows of narrow lights.

And against the wall of the house he built chambers round about, against the walls of the house round about, both of the temple and of the oracle: and he made chambers round about.

The nethermost chamber was five cubits board and the middle was six cubits broad and the third was seven cubits broad: for without in the wall of the house he made narrowed rests round about, the beams should not be fastened in the walls of the house.

And the house, when it was in building, was built of stone made ready before it was brought thither: so that there was neither hammer nor axe nor any tool of iron heard in the house, while it was in building.

The door for the middle chamber was in the right side of the house: and they went up with winding stairs into the middle chamber, and out of the middle into the third.

So he built the house and finished it: and covered the house with beams and boards of cedar. ...

And the whole house he overlaid with gold until he had finished all the house: also the whole altar that was by the oracle he overlaid with gold.

And within the oracle he made two cherubims of olive tree, each ten cubits high.

The two doors also were of the olive tree, and he carved upon them carvings of cherubims and palm trees and open flowers and overlaid them with gold, and spread gold upon the cherubims and upon the palm trees.

So it goes on. Solomon's Temple becomes more and more magnificent. In Arabian storytelling, it is jinns who weave the magic into the Temple. I rather like the more prosaic version of Kings. The construction of the Temple can be read as unlocking of the key to the universe—or a kind of builder's manual. Hiram is revered by the freemasons because he was the builder of the Temple. The masons are practical men as well as God-fearing.

The brotherhood of Freemasons takes their inspiration from the masons who built Solomon's Temple. One of their symbols is two stones side by side, one rough, one smooth. The Temple is also an allegory for personal advancement towards enlightenment. From the rough stone to the smooth stone. This symbol stands in a glass case at Freemason's hall. Rough to smooth: life is a process of attainment and improvement.

The society flourished during the British Empire and reveres the Masonic poems of Rudyard Kipling, written from the Lodge of Hope and Perseverance, in Lahore, Punjab, then India, now Pakistan.

King Solomon's Banquet. Published in 1926.
"Once in so often," King Solomon said,
Watching his quarrymen drill the stone,
We will club our garlic and wine and bread
And banquet together beneath my Throne.
And all the Brethren shall come to that mess
As Fellow-Craftsmen—no more no less.

Send a swift Shallop to Hiram of Tyre,
Felling and floating our beautiful trees,
Say that the Brethren and I desire
Tale with our Brethren who use the seas.
And we shall be happy to meet them as mess
As Fellow-Craftsmen—no more no less.

Carry this message to Hiram Abif-
Excellent Master of forge and mine;
I and the Brethren would like it if
He and the Brethren will come to dine,
(Garments from Bozrah or morning dress)
As Fellow Craftsmen—no more no less.
God gave the Hyssop and Cedar their place—
Also the Bramble, the Fig and the Thorn—
But there is no reason to black a man's face
Because he is not what he hasn't been born,
And, as touching the Temple, I hold and profess,
We are Fellow Craftsmen—no more and no less.

So it was ordered and it was done,
And the hewers of wood and the Masons of Mark
With foc'sle hands of the Sidon run
And Navy Lords from the Royal Art,
Came and sat down and were merry at mess
As Fellow Craftsmen—no more and no less.

The quarries are hotter than Hyram's forge,
No one is safe from the dog-whip's reach.
It's mostly snowing up Lebanon gorge,
And it's always blowing off Joppa beach;
But once in so often, the messenger brings
Solomon's mandate; "Forget these things!"
Brother to Beggars and Fellow to Kings
Companion of Princes—forget these things!
Fellow Craftsmen, forget these things!'

Dr Staples says that there are 6 million Freemasons in the world, who attest to a belief in a Supreme Being. "You need to believe in something outside yourself. You need an external moral reference. You have to have an idea of God. That is where the all-seeing eye comes from."

He regards the founding of America as a giant Masonic experiment based on equality, fraternity and charity. "That was the American constitution."

Today, among the masons, the name of Solomon lives on. The Grand Master's chair is called the Throne of Solomon. The Grand Master represents Solomon. The Grand Master is the Duke of Kent. So, here, 3,000 years on from Solomon, we find the King of ancient Israel represented by a cousin of the Queen of England. It celebrates the power and wisdom of one man. The commanding axis of a woman, the Queen of Sheba, has no resonance here. And I miss her. There are still clubs in London—the Garrick comes to mind—where women are banned from certain areas. I am old enough to have been lectured by men in leather armchairs or grand offices. The entrance of the Queen of Sheba is a turning point for womankind.

Chapter 7

Yorkshire and London,
October The Queen of Sheba Through
the Eyes of a Yorkshire Landowner and
a Bluestocking Dame

I have started to answer some of my hard questions about the Queen of Sheba. I have an idea of where she came from, what she looked like, and what she represented in faith and magic. But I want to know something more personal about her. What was she actually like? What kind of mind did she have? And why does she feel so close?

Everyone has a claim on her, says Eyob. So I shall try to see her through the eyes of some who love her. A Brazilian artist, a Yorkshire landowner, a distinguished academic Dame.

The artist is Ana Maria Pacheco, a sculptor, painter and printmaker who was born in Brazil but has worked mostly in the United Kingdom. She arrives at the National Gallery in London, small, ageless and vivid, with glittering earrings. She has a broad face and dark eyes.

On a puritanical wintry day in London, she exudes the colour of her native Brazil. And when she thinks of the Queen of Sheba she thinks of *Song of Songs* and Flaubert, of exotic gardens and flying carpets. I am struck by something else she says. It was the painting in the National Gallery by Claude Lorrain of the Queen of Sheba embarking on her voyage to Jerusalem which was the start of her artistic journey. She loved the drama of the scene, the expectation and the magnificence of the Queen of Sheba's entourage. But, she says: "The figure of the Queen of Sheba was tiny!"

In other words, it was the journey that is at the centre of the story. It was the encounter in Jerusalem that brought her to life. I feel that I am drawing nearer my own embarkation. Once I have a fuller picture of the Queen of Sheba, I am ready to follow that tiny figure on the grand horizon of possibility.

Ana Maria Pacheco muses on the character of the Queen. Here was a woman who, according to some folk versions, had killed her first tyrant husband. He was a lascivious king who was raping the women of Saba, so she coaxed him into the marriage bed then plunged in the knife. There is no documentary evidence of course, but why was this original husband assigned to her in folklore? She is an avenger of women, flirtatious and ferocious.

Pacheco places her, dressed in white, in an earthly garden of delight. The kingdom of Sheba is almost obscenely luscious. It flows with water and is heavy with spices. Ana Maria Pacheco decided to make this landscape something between Eden and Hieronymus Bosch. Some of the animals appearing in the garden appear fantastic, but Pacheco imagines the whole represented.

Then there is the relationship in the dark Eden between Solomon and Sheba. Pacheco depicts it as a clash between power and matriarchy. Critics have described Pacheco's paintings as 'two utterly powerful people encountering one another', but the artist sees submission. We know that, according to Arab tradition, the Queen of Sheba was tricked into sleeping with Solomon.

The garden of delights is clearly resonant of the garden of Eden, but with a key difference. It is the man who seduces the woman this time. Pacheco is ambivalent about this.

"Power is a neutral force, it can be abused." She points out that female power can be 'destructive' and cites the Queen of the Night from Mozart's Magic Flute. "I think women have a connection with life that escapes men. They can procreate. That is what the Queen of Sheba did. She became the powerful mother."

I love the sexy matriarchal Queen of Sheba of these paintings, but not as much as the person who has bought the paintings. The unlikely admirer is a Yorkshire landowner and Ana Maria Pacheco's modern and unashamedly sexual portraits hang on the walls of a rather traditional, eighteenth-century house in North Yorkshire.

They were bought by the British baronet Sir Richard Storey, a businessman and Conservative Party grandee whose family once owned provincial newspapers. As a countryman who was one of the principal supporters of the campaign for Britain to leave the European Union, he does not immediately seem the type of man to be enchanted by the gorgeous, exotic temptress visualised by Pacheco.

83

I drive up to the North Yorkshire moors in the crisp winter, pausing to visit the astonishing ruins of two twelfth-century Cistercian abbeys, Fountains and Rievaulx. They have an austere, spiritual beauty in the fading, wintry light that fails to prepare me for the explosion of colour and hot passion in Pacheco's work.

From the village of Malton—dressed for Christmas like the set of a Richard Curtis movie—I turn into a landscaped park and park by the stables of Settrington House, now owned by Sir Richard's son and daughter in law. Kenelm Storey greets me warmly and shows me into the large, beautifully proportioned drawing room and two vast canvases, Ana Maria Pacheco's paintings of Solomon and Sheba.

They dominate both the room and the mood of the room. The Queen of Sheba is gleaming black against a white dress that follows her curves, her eyes wide and lips open, one hand on her belly, the other on her hip. Her nipples jut. She is wearing gold jewellery. Solomon looks out from the painting, pale and long-faced, and furtive. He is carrying a blue casket. The couple are in a paradise garden with recognisably British flowers—daffodils, cornflowers, lily of the valley, wild roses—but also exotic creatures—a peacock, a parrot, a white deer or ibex, a porcupine, a monkey.

The painting is called Queen of Sheba and King Solomon in the Garden of Earthly Delights, inspired by *Song of Songs*. Her painting is full of desire, temptation, delight and danger. Critics reflect on the symbolism of the Queen of Sheba's foot treading on the tail of the peacock—subduing pride perhaps—and of the porcupine beneath Solomon, representing lurking danger.

Beneath the portrait, are three panels based on Renaissance altarpieces. They tell their own story. One is of the Queen of Sheba's overthrow of the villainous and lascivious king in her land. She seduces him and decapitates him. He is an absurd, fleshy figure in a breastplate and a crown. She is kneeling before him, hair spread and offering a golden casket. In the neighbouring panel, she is carrying off his head in a basket, at the end of a rod. Her dress is gossamer pink. Her expression, as always, is vivid and led by her eyes.

The English landowner liked this portrait so much that he commissioned a second, The Queen of Sheba and King Solomon in the Hall of Riddles. This time, the Queen of Sheba approaches Solomon from the other side, in a crimson dress, both hands pressing on the folds of her abdomen. Her hair is unruly behind her crown. She looks out from the painting, voluptuous, intelligent, and alert. Solomon looks philosophical, hand on mouth, watching her through hooded eyes. He cannot take his eyes off her. She brings the force of nature, while he has the column and throne, the interior.

It is not just the beauty and tempestuous sexiness that I have come to love about the Queen of Sheba but also that she is also clever, funny and fearless. This queen set off on an intrepid journey into the unknown to find out the truth for herself. She was bold enough to ask questions of the world's most powerful ruler. Our Queen of Sheba is not just the alabaster face of Myriam, that first century AD head found at a cemetery in Yemen and dubbed the south Arabian Mona Lisa. She is a natural intellectual, a role model, a leader of the fun crowd.

Up to now, I have seen her portrayed as a Renaissance figure of blank virtue or as sexy voluptuary. But I learn that the Bloomsbury Group, that early-twentieth-century collection of artists, writers and thinkers, took a different view. The group included the novelist Virginia Woolf, the economist John Maynard Keynes and the intellectual Lytton Strachey.

Another member was Duncan Grant, a cousin of Lytton Strachey and his sister Pernel Strachey, who became a principal of Newnham College, Cambridge. Grant was an impulsive romantic who managed affairs with both Vanessa Bell, sister of Virginia Woolf, and his cousin Lytton Strachey. More complicated still, he also slept with David Garnett, who later married Angelica, the daughter Grant had with Vanessa Bell.

In another career, I interviewed Angelica—striking looking and strangely child-like—when she was in her late eighties, living an artist's life near Aix de Provence in the south of France. As I tried to untangle the relationships of her life, she was both confiding and quick-tempered. She lived and died a bohemian.

The paintings of her father, Duncan Grant, were often influenced by religion and mythology. In 1912, he embarked on a painting intended for Newnham College. The subject he chose was King Solomon and the Queen of Sheba.

The painting is owned by the Tate art gallery but is currently in storage rather than on display. I put in a request to view it and a month or so later I set off to an industrial estate off the New Kent Road, near Elephant and Castle, south London. At the end of corridors and locked rooms is a large, bare, harshly lit room full of steel lockers.

A few paintings are balanced in front of the lockers. And here is the Queen of Sheba, in the oriental costume of baggy trousers, long silk red coat and scarf tied as a turban. Her hands are gesticulating to emphasise a point. Solomon, cheek on hand, wearing a turban, listens intently to her. She has the magnetism of an Arabian storyteller, her hands in a snake-like gesture.

Those who know the Bloomsbury circle immediately recognise that Duncan Grant has modelled Solomon on Lytton Strachey. The Queen of Sheba is unmistakably his sister Pernel. Our great eastern queen has become a pale and angular bluestocking. I marvel again at how the Queen of Sheba can appear in so many guises. Truly, her magnetism exists in the eye of the beholder. She is Ethiopian, or Southern Arabian, she is a fertility symbol, or she is a pinched looking intellectual. Everyone claims her. She is personal. I have not yet decided on my own version of the Queen of Sheba; because I associate her with study and I have so much more to learn.

Perhaps one of the world's oldest universities would be a good setting to try to understand her. Before submitting to a tutorial with our leading academics, I recap the queen's intellectual claims, which are based on the cleverness of her questions. Most of what we know comes from three great works: the Old Testament, the Koran and *The Kebra Nagast* (the glory of kings) a collection of legends brought together in Ethiopia in the fourteenth century to record that the country's rulers were descended from Solomon. We supplement that information with a wealth of folklore, many of it from countries far beyond the Middle East.

The nature of her search—the Queen of Sheba's riddles, goes to the heart of her intelligence. She questions identity, appearance versus reality, she questions God himself.

The riddles she posed to Solomon multiply—responding to the folk tradition of riddles.

"What is the water that comes neither from the earth nor the sky?"

The jinns answer for Solomon: "It is the sweat of horses."

"Now tell me, what colour of the Lord is?" Solomon, in one version of the story, faints at the blasphemy. An angel arrives to intervene.

Her questions go to conventions of hierarchy and gender. There is, for instance, her riddle of gender. She prepared boys and girls of the same height and dressed them identically and tells Solomon to differentiate the sexes. Solomon commands that roasted corns are distributed before them. The boys gather up the corns into their garments. The girls more modestly put them into their headdresses. It turns out to be learned behaviours that distinguish the boys from the girls.

The Queen challenges Solomon again: She brings out a group of boys, some circumcised, some not. Solomon calls the priest to open the Ark of the Covenant. The circumcised bow but the uncircumcised prostrate themselves. Solomon claims that gentiles are theologically more overwhelmed by God's presence. He was addressing a pagan Queen, so this may be a nuanced attempt at converting her. In the Koran, it is more straightforward; she accepts the greater virtue of Suleiman's God.

I am struck by how daunting this must be for her. When Solomon sends his hoopoe bird to Kitor, the Queen is praying to the rising sun. Its light is blocked out by Solomon's force filling the sky. The Queen is full of anguish and begins tearing at her garment. Then she reads his letter:

From me: Solomon the King who sends greetings. Peace unto you and your nobles Queen of Sheba! No doubt you are aware that the Lord of the Universe has made me king of the beasts of the field, the birds of the sky, and the demons, spirits and Liliths. All the kings of the East and West and North and South come to me and pay homage. If you would come and greet me I will honour you more than any kingly guest of mine. But if you refuse and do not appear before me to pay homage I will send out against you my generals contingents and riders.

You ask, "What generals, contingents and riders has King Solomon?" Then know that the beasts of the field are my generals, the birds in the sky are my riders and the demons, spirits and Liliths are my contingents who will strangle you in your beds. The beasts will slay you in the fields and the birds of the sky will consume your flesh.

Men! After reading this, the Queen of Sheba assembles her advisers and asks for advice. They suggest she ignore the letter, which sounds like putting your head in the sand. But the Queen of Sheba does not. She decides to confront Solomon—and with magnificence, rather than subservience or her own armies. "She assembled all the ships of her domain and loaded them with presents for Solomon—pearls and precious stones."

She also presents him with 6,000 young boys and girls, each born at exactly the same time. When she arrives, she finds the King seated in a room of glass. She raises her dress to cross what she thought was water. Solomon says to her: "You're a beautiful woman but hairiness is for men. You look absolutely disgraceful."

She has unnerved him with her challenge to gender. Then she begins wordplay: "What is it? A basin of wood and pail of iron; it draws stones but pours out water."

The answer is a cosmetic box. It is a feminine reference and he answers unhesitatingly. Two can play at this game.

"It comes as dust from the earth and it feeds on dust. It is poured like water but lights the house? What is it? Flax." Flax is one of the exports of Saba, so she may be trading here.

There is curious evidence of Ben Sira, a Hellenistic Jewish scribe and allegorist from Jerusalem, dated second century BC. Sira is in the tradition of Rabbinic narratives from Hebrew literature. He writes of an imagined game of wits between himself and Nebuchadnezzar, the King of Babylon, who conquers Jerusalem in 586 BC. Nebuchadnezzar sends for Ben Sira, in the story, and Sira sends back a rabbit "Delivered as promised, one of the beasts of the field to serve you."

Nebuchadnezzar, it is claimed in the story, is the offspring of King Solomon and the queen of Sheba. Nebuchadnezzar asks why the head of the rabbit is smooth, and Sira responds: "It is a miracle in lime. But if you really want to know, ask your mother."

It is a pretty slanderous allegation to claim that the Queen of Sheba is the mother of the destroyer of Jerusalem. It would also cast her into the gallery of vengeful Bible women—Jezebel, Delilah, or Jael who kills the Canaanite king Sisera by driving a stake through his head so hard it comes out the other side. He falls beneath her legs, the final sexual metaphor.

In his book: *Demonising the Queen of Sheba: Boundaries of Gender and Culture in Postbiblical Judaism and Medieval Islam*, Jacob Lassner challenges the depiction of the "Sheban queen who acts like a man and presumes to rule over them."

He calls her a 'quintessential seductress': her loyalty cannot be taken for granted, she is foreign and she is lethal. She is in fact a composite of the dangerous women feared by men.

The oral tradition brings her vividly to life—a woman of sense and passion, human but related to the spirits, a diplomat, a trader, a lover. In art, she is both merry and transcendent. Women admire her, everyone desires her. She stands for light but also darkness. In Jewish legend, she becomes a night demon, and by the Middle Ages, she was also Lilith. So she is both associated with the fertility goddess Asherah, and with Lilith, a strangler of babies.

Lilith was Adam's original wife who preceded the creation of Eve. She refused to recognise her husband's status and demanded sexual equality. She insisted on reversing sexual positions and mounting him. She said the name Yahweh out loud and threatened to harm new infants. Her threat was to the order of the universe itself. The Queen of Sheba is not shrill and she wears her power tactfully, but the hairy legs are a sign of danger.

She is the mother of Menelik, so fount of divine monarchy, but according to Jesus ben Sira, author of Ecclesiasticus, mother of Nebuchadnezzar. In both cases, she can be said to be the destroyer of Jerusalem. The Ark of the Covenant was stolen and brought to Ethiopia—Jerusalem was sacked by the Babylonians. She is creative and she is destructive.

In at least one story, the Queen of Sheba is a straightforward witch, who comes to question Solomon so that she can better employ serpents to do her bidding. In one folk tale, the Queen of Sheba has golden hair so long it has to be carried in a bowl by a handmaiden. She promises a male admirer gold each day, so long as he keeps their encounters secret. When her suitor's wife follows them she takes back her wealth and strangles his children. The Queen of Sheba is mighty, but she is not merciful.

This view of women is both old and new. Women who disrupt the status quo are attacking the male hegemony of Western civilisation. Look at the Knight Templars, followers of Solomon. In the fourteenth-century depictions of Solomon, he resembles a priest. The Templars represent rationality, obedience, the life of the mind. See how the masonic order appears in Mozart's Magic Flute, and how it subdues the crafty hysteria of the Queen of the Night.

Look how today, intellectuals such as Jordan Peterson still claim that chaos is represented by 'the feminine' and order is 'masculine'. The hairiness of the Queen of Sheba's legs becomes a symbol of obscene lust for power.

From hairy legs, manhood is not far off. There is a Polish tale, recorded in Israel, of boys playing on banks of the river. A voice calls out to them: "Boys, boys, Come to me and I shall you give you lovely things." The boys see a figure in the water, with a pipe in their mouth. It is the Queen of Sheba in disguise. They approach her, she snatches them and pulls them into the water. This is the worst-case against the Queen of Sheba. She has usurped men. The hairy legs, the goat's foot and the sexual appetite are clear signs that she has upset the natural order.

The cultural historian Marina Warner has studied what she terms the erotic meaning of the riddles and the influence of the Queen of Sheba from the tales of Arabia to Jamaica, where the Rastafarians still love her and respect the Solomonic dynasty.

It is charming to imagine Marina Warner, a pixie faced bluestocking in her seventies, her hair piled high, with grey/brown strands falling around her face, standing outside Bob Marley's house in order to absorb the connection with the Queen of Sheba.

I visit her at her home at the end of a row of pretty terraced houses in north London. The house is tall and narrow and there are books everywhere. We sit at her kitchen table where she opens a file on the Queen of Sheba—cuttings, her programme for a short children's opera on the subject, which still makes her chuckle. The children adored it, it was slightly naughty. They all sang the song: 'We want to see the Queen of Sheba's legs'.

What attracted Warner to the Queen of Sheba was not especially her beauty, but that she was a wordsmith: "In the text is she is wealthy, powerful and apparently has this sharp mind. And she is associated with riddling knowledge. The hard questions of the bible turn into riddles. And there you have a connection with figures like the Sphinx.

"Riddles are deep in all philosophies and religions and very widely spread in folklore, African folklore. It is a method of teaching wisdom. The mainspring of a riddle is that the first meaning is not the right one."

The riddle which most intrigues Marina Warner is the one about the boys and the roasted corn. What does it mean that the boys scoop them up while girls go down on their knees to gather them up for their headdresses? For Solomon, kneeling and modesty are for the female sex. I remember what Eyob told me about the Ethiopian depiction of the Queen of Sheba. She does not kneel before Solomon. She is equal.

Warner writes in her book on depictions of women *From the Beast to the Blonde*: "The encounter between Solomon and Sheba was thus recounted as a battle of the sexes as well as a battle of wits and the challengers faced each other not only to determine the truth and errors of their gods but the respective mettle of their minds."

King trumps queen, but remember how the story ends. Solomon eventually becomes a figure of hubris and lasciviousness and a worshipper of false gods. He loses his kingdom. And, according to *The Kebra Nagast* at least, the Queen of Sheba has a final trick up her sleeve, which is allowing her son by Solomon, Menelik, to bring the Ark of the Covenant to Ethiopia.

This we know of the Queen of Sheba. Her riddles had dual meanings. In versions of the tale, she walked over a pond made of glass. She asked Solomon to guess the gender of her entourage. Nothing is what it seems. Mirrors are deceptive but also a means of revelation. To quote John Dee, English mathematician to Queen Elizabeth I, when we see "the creatures of God, both in the heavens above and in the earth beneath… as in a glasse, we beholde the exceeding maiestie and wisdome of God."

There is a playful quality to her riddles, but they also touch on deeper themes. She is confronting Solomon, who has the gift of wisdom. She is trying to understand, perhaps, the divine enigma behind this.

Eleanor Cook, an English professor at the University of Toronto, has made a study of the Queen of Sheba's riddles. Riddles, or hard questions, are a route to understanding. The Queen of Sheba is in the tradition of the Sphinx and the Griffin. In the Grecian form, the Sphinx is tripartite, the head of a woman, the body of a lion and the wings of a bird.

Eleanor Cook quotes the second-century Christian theologian Clement of Alexandria on the role of sphinxes in front of Egyptian temples. They were there to show "that discussion about God is enigmatic and obscure." The Word of God is therefore an enigma. The *Book of Revelation* says: "I am Alpha and Omega, the first and the last."

No wonder John Donne, the celebrated sixteenth-/seventeenth-century cleric and love poet wrote of man's difficulty in getting to the bottom of things: "Poore intricated soule! Riddling, perplexed, labyrinthicall soul!"

Was there another reason that the Queen of Sheba was distrusted? Marina Warner, looking into the distance in her book-lined room, understands the burden. In the court of Solomon, the Queen of Sheba was an incomer: "And she comes from the south. It has become even stronger; a lot of the revulsion against migration is migration from the south. The south is associated with luxury and indolence. Corruption."

Foreign and clever and feared.

I realise that the Queen of Sheba was a purveyor of riddles and a riddle herself. And I am sure that the clue for me is in the Claude Lorrain painting. It is time for me to start planning my journey.

Chapter 8

Portsmouth, November Preparing to Set Sail in the Style of the Queen of Sheba

I am confident now that I have a queen, with roots in Ethiopia and southern Arabia and Egypt. I have an expensive and internationally popular commodity, which is frankincense. I have, in Jerusalem, a great city and a mighty king, though it is possible that the glory of these last two may have been more talked up by later generations than a reality of the time. The celebrated embassy to Jerusalem, the glamorous meeting of a king and queen, begins to make sense for three reasons: sex, politics and trade.

But how did she get there? Previous investigations about Solomon and Sheba have imagined her on a journey by land, crossing several hundred miles of inhospitable sand dunes. The caravan routes of the time are documented. But wouldn't the trip have been more comfortably undertaken by sea? The eastern promontory of the Red Sea would take a sailor to Aqaba—close to Eilat, on what is now a border between Jordan and Israel—from where it is another 200 miles to Jerusalem.

It would make sense, would it not, for her to make the journey by sea and then by camel or horse?

I call Eyob to ask him another central question. What would have been the best time of year for her to travel?

He says that 11 September is the day that her return is celebrated. It is called Enkutatash, and it is the first day of the New Year in Ethiopia. The date marks the end of the rain season. According to tradition, the celebration goes back to the time when the Queen of Sheba returned to Ethiopia from her long visit to King Solomon, she was received with great joy and her people gave her a Pearl. Enkutatash means 'pearl for your difficult journey'. A pearl for a difficult journey, of course.

If she returns in September, I reckon she must have set sail in spring. It was a long journey, she had a great entourage, and she was entertained in style in Jerusalem so would not have hurried away. And she was there long enough to conceive a child.

If I am to master her journey, I know that I shall have to try to understand the Red Sea winds which govern all voyages.

These depend on the seasonal cycle of the Indian Ocean monsoons. Between June and September, the winds are from the north in the Red Sea, while the southwest monsoon is in the Indian Ocean. During the winter season, southern winds are in the Red Sea while the northeast monsoon blows in the Indian Ocean. There are also local winds. It is calmest in August and September which would have made the Queen of Sheba's return most pleasant, especially if she were suffering from morning sickness.

Next, I must contemplate the route. Would she have hugged the shore, rising pirates and reefs, or launched down the central channel, as large boats do today?

There is one famous ancient maritime expedition to compare the voyage to. It was a celebrated launch by an Egyptian Pharoah to bring back treasures from a fabled land. It was called the expedition of Punt.

I decide I must consult Kathryn Bard, the American who excavated Mersa Gawasis harbour in Egypt. She is an expert maritime archaeologist and expert on the Punt expedition, the boat sent down the Red Sea by Egypt's Queen Hatshepsut almost 1,500 years before Christ was born to bring gold, frankincense and other treasures. The exact location of Punt is debated but is thought by many to have been what now Ethiopia is. Ms Bard has been at pains, over the years, to differentiate her painstaking work in Egypt from the drama of the Hollywood movie *Raiders of the Lost Ark*. I fear she may not have a high opinion of the media's grasp of archaeology.

She answers the phone, but cuts short my hypothetical question on the Queen of Sheba's route: "She could not have travelled anywhere because she was fictitious."

I feel there is too big a story here to allow the queen to be laid to rest so cruelly. "But if she had, would it have been more likely by boat or by land?"

Bard is adamant. Frankly, it would have been neither. There is historical evidence that Egyptian ports were closed during the tenth century BC because of war. For the same reasons, overland journeys were unlikely. This is not going well. Could she allow the possibilities of a voyage on boats or journey on camels laden with gold and frankincense? Bard responds with exasperated laughter: "No because the Queen of Sheba was fictitious." Her parting shot is especially withering. If anyone had been travelling overland at this time it would more likely have been by donkey than on a camel. This has never been the image I had of the queen entering Jerusalem.

But Dr Iris Gerlach has given me hope again. How do you explain those painted reliefs of the Punt expedition, painted around the time to decorate the Temple of Hatshepsut in Luxor in Egypt? They show a line of fishes beneath the boat. "What do you notice?" asked Dr Gerlach. "These are sea fishes. Would the Queen of Sheba have gone by sea then?"

"Why not? Technically it would have been possible. And she was a Queen!"

She was a queen, and I feel less bad about being sent packing by Kathryn Bard. Surely, ships would have suited her better than donkeys. I build my theory using the work of the Portuguese Jesuit Nicolao Godinho, who published De Abassinorum Rebus in 1615. Godinho cited the story of the claimed royal descent from Solomon and the Queen of the south or Queen of Sheba. In Godinho's version, the queen departed from Ethiopia, via the Eritrean coast and the Arabian Gulf and reached Jerusalem in eight days. There was clearly a seafaring tradition in the Red Sea.

We know that the prevailing winds are from the north. That would make it much harder for her journey to Jerusalem than her return. She could have hugged the coast but would have had to be mindful of reefs and rocks.

As for tacking—working the sails back and forth—to deal with the winds, he does not think the Queen's crew would have known how to do it. The Romans worked it out some years later. On the other hand, we know she took plenty of soldiers with her, so they could have rowed when the sailing was rough. Ah yes, the soldiers. Our Queen of Sheba is peaceable and diplomatic, but the soldiery of the time had a fearsome reputation.

The incense route became crucial in the ninth century BC. Since the dates for the Queen of Sheba are misty, we could think of moving here a century. A possible route would be from Dhofar, now in southern Oman, to Adulis in Eritrea and up to Dedan in what is now Saudi Arabia.

She could have travelled along the King's Highway through Jordan, into Jerusalem.

So she could have gone by sea or by a combined sea and land route. The Queen of Sheba was not a desert queen and would not naturally have been equipped to make the journey that way. Yemenis were settled people, who used to water from monsoons and made their living through agriculture and trade. They are not nomads.

How long would such a voyage take? Our seventeenth-century Jesuit Nicolao Godinho whisks her up there in eight days, which seems a little fast for the time. I consult a man who would have a good idea of speed, Sir Robin Knox-Johnston. Between June 1968 and April 1969, he became the first man to sell single-handedly around the world without stopping, a feat no one had been sure was possible. Sir Robin, the unseen hero of the film *The Mercy*, about the death of the British yachtsman Donald Crowhurst in that same race, has had an astonishing life of adventure. He approaches my maritime challenge with enthusiasm and imaginative determination.

"In summer, it would have been more than thirty-five degrees on the bridge at night—she wouldn't have been able to sleep," says Knox-Johnston, recreating her on the spot, although I have sprung the seafaring puzzle on him without warning.

Sir Robin speculates that the Queen of Sheba would have sailed and used rowers. I ask about dangerous reefs and he says that he will have to consult his Admiralty maps. How long does he think her sea journey would have lasted? Sir Robin is more cautious. "It is going to be—depends on the wind—assume they could row. Viking ships could do 120 miles a day—about 50, 60 miles a day rowing. About 4 weeks?"

If the boat were heavily laden with spices and treasures that would have slowed her down. There is also a micro-climate to the Red Sea which is influenced by the monsoons of India, which might have dragged her further. She would have sailed on a dhow, the traditional sailing vessel used in the Red Sea and the Indian Ocean.

With their long, hulls, dhows could carry heavy goods along the coasts. The Queen of Sheba may have had a fleet of them.

As for the wood used for the ship, I ask if the famous cedar from Lebanon that supplied Solomon's Temple could have been traded down the Red Sea. Sir Robin prefers to think of it coming from India. "Certainly, Saudi is not famous for its forests." And oars? "They would have had those—simple, long pole with a paddle on the end."

His greater concern is the quality of her quarters. Sir Robin says that women used to be pushed down below—"Poor things!"—and he likes to think of the Queen of Sheba set up on deck: "It would have been like the Egyptians."

Sir Robin is by now playfully engaged in this journey. "Sounds a bit of fun—the dhows to look out for—haven't changed hugely in a thousand years. They are good sea boats. Three thousand years ago more primitive, no deck and more open. Viking trading ships, not long boats, covered using skins."

There is another reason for giving the Queen of Sheba a voyage. I remember the Dean of Canterbury Cathedral guiding me towards the meaning of her journey. The sea is revered as a sacred place. It was the narrative of creation; life came from the sea.

Let us look at the Red Sea conditions for boats during antiquity. I turn to the university of Naples professor Chiara Zazzaro. His paper has looked at how tides, currents and winds affect maritime routes. The Red Sea is about 2,300 km from what is now the Suez Canal to the Bab el-Mandeb Strait, between Yemen and Eritrea. Within this stretch, there was a flourishing maritime trade between the Mediterranean and the Indian Ocean—it formed the great spice route.

The professor navigated the north-western stretch of the Red Sea in a reconstructed Pharaonic craft. He also established the depth of the Red Sea basin. A boat at the time of the Queen of Sheba would have kept sight of the coast, keeping a careful lookout for dangerous coral reefs. The first-century sailors' manual Periplus Maris Erythraei describes the coastal landmarks.

Chiara Zazzaro writes: "The favourable sailing conditions, the presence of thousands of small islands providing stopping points for navigation, and the proximity of the African and Arabian coasts probably encouraged navigation from an early date, perhaps in order to reach sources of products, such as obsidian—a volcanic glass—to exchange goods or indeed out of mere curiosity."

Professor Zazzaro notes that Edulis harbour in Eritrea was the gateway for the Red Sea and Indian Ocean trade. Not much is known about Edulis before the first century AD, although ware pottery found at Edulis suggests that settlers were there in the first millennium BC and that there was a trade linking Egypt, Sudan and South Arabia. Ivory was definitely exported from the Edulis region by sea to India, Persia and Rome. Elephants were recorded as disappearing from North Africa in the first century AD.

Trade is the key to the world of the Queen of Sheba. If I can crack the trade route, the revelations will come.

The excitement of the Indian Ocean Red Sea trade is the potential it gives for suggesting things were going on much earlier than we first thought. Whereas it had been assumed to be prospering in the second century AD, more recent research suggests the late first millennium BC. Ceramics from Arabia, Aksum,

South Arabia and India at places across the western Indian Ocean are more historically accurate. We are edging a bit closer to the Queen of Sheba.

The maritime logs of Periplus of the Erythraean Sea, dated from the first centuries AD, give us a picture of the Red Sea as a hub of trade, bringing precious stones and incense to service Egyptian Pharaohs. The African coast benefited, the kingdom of Abyssinia rivalling the 'frankincense state' of Southern Arabia. This was the era in which Rome conquered Egypt—ending with Cleopatra. The Red Sea route became vital.

So, naturally, I want to get up the Red Sea too, but this is tricky. It is not a tourist route, for the waters are perilously prone to piracy. In my days as a newspaper reporter, I have visited Djibouti, spending some time aboard a British naval ship. Some months later, in 2007, Royal Navy personnel travelling in a launch from the same vessel, HMS Cornwall, were surrounded by Iranian Revolutionary Guards and briefly detained off the Iran coast. These are dangerous waters.

I email my favourite admiral, Lord West, to ask if there is any chance of hitching a ride. I get a sympathetic but pained reply:

Dear Sarah,
One of the sad facts about the steady erosion of our Navy by successive governments is the scarcity of UK warships around the world.
If you had asked me this when I was Commander in Chief in 2002 then I could probably have arranged something, but now much more difficult. We do however still try to keep a presence in the Horn of Africa and in the Gulf.
Eritrea can be tricky for access, as we don't regularly visit.
I will raise with the present First Sea Lord, but it is quite an ask and I think it is unlikely. Ministers would be interested and the FCO (Foreign and Commonwealth office) would also be involved. The movement /location of a warship has a diplomatic significance.

Yours aye,
Alan

This is a blow. The tourist boats in the Red Sea stay firmly in the Gulf of Aqaba. I start to look into commercial vessels while investigating the history of maritime expeditions from Edulis up to the gulf.

Then I receive a second email from the navy, this time from Captain James Dean, of the First Sea Lord's office:

Dear Sarah,

As you know, Admiral Lord West undertook to contact this office on the subject of your request for support to the southern Red Sea leg of your Queen of Sheba quest. I thought I would send this short message to confirm I have received his email and to let you know that I have passed your request to the team in Navy Command HQ that plans ships deployments to ascertain whether there is any way we might be able to support you.

I will let you know as soon as I can what, if any, options might exist but please do feel free to use me as your point of contact in the meantime or for any other related matters.

Yours,
James Dean

I cannot tell if this is Navy language for not a hope and I start to look at other routes. We could put the Queen of Sheba on her donkey and take her through Egypt or through Saudi Arabia. But I have become attached to the notion of her taking a great boat filled with incense, gold and animals. A few weeks later I hear again from Captain Dean:

Dear Sarah,

As promised, and with apologies for the delay in responding to your request, my enquiries have revealed that we will likely have a ship in the area in question, but not until late March. I regret I can't confirm at this range whether, where or when she might conduct any port visits that would facilitate your recording but if you think that time frame could still work—noting I think you were seeking something a bit earlier in the year—then please let me know and I can examine the options in more detail.

I am sorry I can't be clearer but operational tasking is always dynamic and I have to be cryptic for reasons of operational security concerning which unit might be available and its movements.

I hope this is helpful to some degree.

Regards,
James

A warship in March is exactly what I am looking for! This is as near as I can get to reconstructing the journey of the Queen of Sheba.

There is one ominous cloud on the horizon—a note from Admiral West noting that one of the navy's ships—HMS Albion—has upset the Chinese by straying on a path in the South China Sea. Not another Suez! Will the warship earmarked for the Red Sea now have to deploy elsewhere. The movement of British ships around the world is now personally relevant to me and I am watching them as if I were Napoleon Bonaparte.

If I am to trace the Queen of Sheba's route up the Red Sea, I better learn some rudimentary lessons of navigation. On a cold, clear winter morning, I catch a train from London to Portsmouth, home of the Royal Navy, the shipyard that built its first warship in 1497. There in the dock is the British navy's latest warship, Queen Elizabeth, a 65,000 tonne, £3.3 billion aircraft carrier recently returned from a goodwill trip to the United States. A visible statement of military power.

Nearby is the smaller, sleeker destroyer HMS Diamond, sibling of HMS Dragon, which is currently on deployment in the Arabian Gulf on counter-terrorism and anti-terrorism duties. The crafts that sail on it have become more deadly, but the Red Sea is as much a battleground for competing powers as it was in the tenth century BC.

Today it is the new power that is Saudi Arabia that takes the lead in regional affairs, not least in its military support to the Yemen government in the civil war against Houthi rebels, a conflict that has brought humanitarian disaster.

At a summit in Riyadh, the Saudi capital, leaders from the Horn of Africa including Djibouti, Sudan and Somalia met to discuss a Red Sea security alliance. Saudi is planning a military base in Djibouti. The United Arab Emirates already has a military base in Eritrea. The Saudis helped broker the peace treaty between Ethiopia and Eritrea. The Gulf states are strategically interested in Ethiopia. The Horn of Africa is mainly Muslim and looks as naturally across the

Red Sea to Arabia as south to the rest of Africa. Just as 3,000 years ago, trade and migration are linked to southern Arabia.

The navigator I meet is Lt Cdr Adam Egeland-Jensen, a modest, tough, pale-skinned and milky haired man in his fifties whose ancestry is Norwegian. Naturally, he cites the Viking Age, which reached its height in the eighth century AD, as evidence that galley ships with strong rowers can be stitched together from planks of wood. Their instruments of navigation included the sun compass and a sunstone.

This would have been simpler east to west than the Queen of Sheba's route south to north, but Makeda/Bilqis set out to Jerusalem as a pagan worshipper of the sun, so would have had a strong relationship with its presence. The Norwegian explorer Thor Heyerdahl undertook the Ra expedition in 1970 sailing from the west coast of Africa to Barbados in a papyrus reed boat. The boat was named after the Egyptian sun god and the reed came from Lake Tana in Ethiopia—part of the Queen of Sheba's domain. Simple boats can survive journeys, particularly in the relative calm of the Red Sea. Her journey if from the Gulf of Aden would have been just over a thousand miles.

Navy ships have sophisticated GPS systems now, but navigators are still trained to be able to establish geographical coordinates by the simplest means. Adam Egeland demonstrates with a piece of string and a square of card how a navigator might plot the celestial system. The lower edge aligns with the horizon and the upper edge the elevation of the star. The knots are finger width apart. Indeed the finger is the simplest system of navigation.

He holds first the string in his mouth and pulls it arm's length, one eye narrowed, and then holds his forefinger up in the same line. He can measure from this the horizon and the sun. The Queen of Sheba would have not have known about longitude and latitude. It took Eratosthenes in the third century BC and Hipparchus in the second century BC to devise a system of time that was not local. But the sun could have been measured at noon, the skies would have been mostly clear and a simple plumb line could have been dropped into the water to determine depth. Local pilots or fishermen would have advised on currents and rocks and reefs.

Adam Egeland approaches the Queen of Sheba's journey with imaginative relish. Trigonometry, the study of lengths and angles, was understood in the Arab world, although dominant in the Hellenistic period of the third century BC. Egeland is sure that the educated maritime culture of Saba would make good use of it. As for the route—the distance between Djibouti on the African continent and the Arabian coast is only about ten miles. The Queen of Sheba could have set out from either side, the Horn of Africa or Southern Arabia. The simplest route is straight up the centre, but she would have moored each night on the coast. There was no Suez Canal before 1869, so no route into the Mediterranean. The seasonal winds require local navigational knowledge.

There are, unsurprisingly, no maps at the naval base library in Portsmouth that helps us with the tenth century BC, but the Admiralty librarian of twenty years, Jennifer Wraight, shows willingness with the romance of maritime history. Ms Wraight is a slim woman, fine hair caught up in a clip, glasses and an earned smile that defies her severity. Her deportment suggests she might walk around the library with volumes of Trafalgar balanced on her head. She is precise in her speech and her actions, with suppressed pride in the depth of her knowledge. Among Ms Wraight's duties is to pick presents for visiting heads of state and she has a keen sense of the particular.

She has a map of Scotland in mind that is relevant to the ancestry of President Trump, for instance. She knows with dignitaries of the Middle East you need to be sensitive to historic names and borders. The Sultan of Brunei would not like the mention of the Persian Gulf. The gift she sourced for Oman was a celestial Atlas containing a star named by the Arabians.

The Admiralty Hydrographic office was set up in 1800 and early charts were printed from copper plates. The context was the commercial interests of the British East India Company and its competition with the Dutch. The company's Royal Charter was given by Elizabeth 1 in 1600 in the great age of exploration, undertaken by the Portuguese, the Spanish and the Dutch. The names of the great maritime explorers are revered by naval folk. Captains are still nicknamed Vasco after Vasco da Gama, the sixteenth-century Portuguese explorer who was the first European to reach India by sea.

Jennifer Wraight has laid out some historic charts and books on tables. I am wide-eyed as she picks them up, and I ask why she does not wear gloves. These are the sorts of questions she enjoys. Because cotton can get fibres onto the page. "Clean, dry hands are best," she nods.

These are examples of what is in front of me:

Atlas of skeleton charts
For the direction and force of winds and currents, and other phenomena, in the Arabian Sea, the Red Sea.

By Alexander Keith Johnston
(London 1854)

Johnston (1804–1871) was a Scottish geographer and cartographer, who combined cartography with a painstaking and scholarly approach to map production. He went on to establish a reputation for scope and accuracy. Thematic atlases became the hallmark of the company he had founded and W and AK Johnston were appointed engravers to King William IV in 1834. In 1835, he constructed the first English language physical globe of the world incorporating its geology, hydrography and meteorology.

Earlier still was Le Neptune Oriental, a nautical map of the southern Red Sea drawn by the French navigator and cartographer Jean-Baptiste-Nicolas-Denis d' Après de Mannevillette in 1775. The detailed chart, with its depth soundings and profiles, was a source of national pride.

Inside an environmental storage room, where the temperature and humidity are regulated are even more beloved treasures, including the atlas of Admiral Nelson's sailing master, Thomas Atkinson, featuring the Battle of the Nile. This was the naval battle between the British and the French in 1798.

Just as engaging, are the Admiralty's collection of early charts and biblical maps. For instance, *The Theatre of the Whole World* by Abraham Ortelius in the sixteenth century, with its pictures of dhows and elephants and sea monsters in the Arabian ocean, and beautiful coloured calligraphy from Arabia Felix. Then there is the fabled kingdom of Prester John.

Most intriguing is the map of William Whiston's description of his models of the tabernacle of Moses: and of Solomon's, Zorobabel's, Herod's and Ezekiel's temples at Jerusalem. Whiston was an acquaintance of Sir Isaac Newton—whom we know was fascinated by Solomon's Temple—and succeeded him as Professor of Mathematics at Cambridge in 1702. He shared the religious beliefs of his predecessor. In 1726, Whiston had models made of the Ark of the Covenant and the Temple of Jerusalem and lectured on them around the country.

But we are digressing. This is the problem with exploring the Queen of Sheba. There are so many different avenues to explore.

The date of my planned naval trip up the Red Sea approaches. British politics in the run-up to Brexit becomes increasingly shaky. The Chancellor of the Exchequer prepares to go to China to boost trade for when the UK seeks deals outside the EU.

The trip is called off because the Chinese are offended by remarks by the Defence Secretary, Gavin Williamson about sending our aircraft carriers to the South China Sea. Coincidentally, I receive an email from the navy, saying HMS Dragon is now 'on task' in the Gulf, so my trip begins to look less likely.

But then, delight! I have the go-ahead to book flights, with my BBC colleague Lauren Harvey, to join Dragon on 15 March at Salahah in Southern Oman. Southern Arabia is a scene of trade and diplomacy now, as it was in the time of the Queen of Sheba. Britain has just signed a military pact with the Sultan Qaboos, which will allow our aircraft carriers to dock in the new port of Duqm, south of Muscat. This will be Britain's first permanent army base east of Suez since 1971.

Oman has become a pivotal broker in the Middle East. It has opposed the role of Saudi Arabia and the UAE in supporting the Yemen Government against Houthi rebels. But it is stopping arms being smuggled through Oman by the rebels.

Muscat was the location for meetings between Iranian officials and Hillary Clinton and John Kerry before President Obama's nuclear deal in 2015.

Then, last October, the Israeli Prime Minister Binyamin Netanyahu came to meet Sultan Qaboos in Muscat. By January, Mike Pompeo, President Trump's Secretary of State arrived there. Oman is determined to be a peacemaker. It is an autocracy but allows social and religious tolerance. It sounds, in fact, a lot like Saba.

I pop into a London office for a cup of coffee with a former British government security official who has a deep affection for the country. He has named his company after the hoopoe bird—or hudhud as it is also called. He tells me that the Koranic text describes the hoopoe returning from Saba with 'certain information' for King Solomon about the Queen of Sheba. Thus, the hoopoe bird remains a symbol for intelligence services in this region.

He also shows me, with some excitement, a photograph of the Sultan Qaboos Grand Mosque in Muscat. The marble floor has a mirrored quality that reflects the buildings and figures above it. Is this the type of Islamic that which could have inspired the tale of a glass floor at Solomon's palace, which the Queen of Sheba mistook for water, thus lifting her skirts?

By now I am eagerly plotting the route that HMS Dragon is likely to take from Oman, heading north up the Gulf of Suez to the Suez Canal and through to the Mediterranean. The canal would amaze the writer of the Periplus, but our first-century Greek-speaking sailor would recognise most of the rest today. He

103

would certainly recognise the route HMS Dragon will take along the coast of Oman and Yemen and through the Bab el Mandeb, where Africa reaches for the Arabian Peninsula.

But there is a trip I must make first. Iris Gerlach is in Yeha, in Ethiopia, excavating a site that will reveal wonderful new clues about the Queen of Sheba. She invites me to go. And of course, I ask Eyob to come with me. He has not seen Yeha nor Axum and I am delighted to see these ancient places through his eyes.

Chapter 9
Ethiopia, December Ethiopian Hunt for the Queen of Sheba

I land in Addis Ababa, a little weary after an overnight flight from London but immediately brighten at the contours of this country and the friendliness of these people. The demure dress and flashing eyes of the stewardess remind me that the feminist spirit does not always have to appear in western dress.

I look at the line of Air Ethiopia planes lined up on the tarmac. One is named The Queen of Sheba. The diplomat and peacemaker. The woman who went to discover other countries. It also shows the capriciousness of borders—the Axumite empire spread to Eritrea as well as Ethiopia.

My search for the Queen started here in Africa with the thoughtful nun in Axum. As I learned more about this monarch from 3,000 years ago, it was clear I would have to come back. The Queen of Sheba is responsible for a royal dynasty in Ethiopia that ended only with the toppling of Emperor Haile Selassie in 1974. Her son with Solomon was brought the country its greatest treasure, the Ark of the Covenant. She was the creative force behind Ethiopia's religiosity and its tradition of hidden knowledge.

It is wonderful serendipity—the kind of magic in which Ethiopia is said to specialise that Iris Gerlach, the archaeologist who was so helpful to me in Berlin, will be visiting the Yeha dig and that Eyob is able to accompany me there. Iris enthused me with her account of the increasing evidence of a Sabaean kingdom that stretched across the sea, encompassing the Horn of Africa and southern Arabia, Ethiopia and Yemen.

Addis is dusty and the air is close. Right now it is waiting for the Old Testament storm that breaks in the evening. Because of its position near the equator, it has an all year balance of twelve hours of the night, twelve hours of the day. It is a bustling, increasingly modern city that looks to the future with ambitious construction projects and to the past with uncontrolled traffic and street traders. Some of the architectural visions—gleaming Dubai style hotels and offices—look a little way off. Rush hour is every hour. It is also devout: I notice people taking the time to sit in contemplation on the steps of the many churches.

Tariku, the young guide who shows me around, welcomes me by saying that it is neither the day nor the year that I think it is. Ethiopia operates on the Julian calendar, proposed by Julius Caesar in 46 BC, rather than the Gregorian calendar, named after Pope Gregory XIII in 1582 and the most widely used. In fact, Ethiopia rather makes up its own rules, starting the year on 11 September. It occurs to me that if the Coptics are making their own calculation on the date of Jesus, perhaps it explains why the Queen of Sheba's dates are so hard to pin down. She took to heart the maxim that a woman should never reveal her age.

Or, perhaps like the fabled figure of Prester John, she is ageless. Prester John illustrates Ethiopia's ability to generate myths. He was believed to have been a priest-king who ruled a bejewelled kingdom, where unicorns roamed. A letter circulated among the leaders of Europe in 1160 describing an early paradise, where there existed a fountain of youth that allowed Prester John to reign for hundreds of years. In 1221, it was reported that Prester John had conquered Persia and was on his way to save Jerusalem.

A Bishop in the Holy Land wrote: 'He is King David of India'. Adventurers and believers claimed Prester John as King of Ethiopia, although none found him. Ethiopia has been called the land of the Queen of Sheba, the land of Prester John, the Land of Punt, that last being the country that was the subject of fabled expeditions by the Egyptians, 3,000 years ago. Like Jerusalem, it is an idea as well as geography.

Tariku says something else which makes me prick up. He says that his tribe people Afro-Asiatic, with a sense of genealogy derived from the Red Sea. There may be something called a Sabaean character and sense of nationhood.

We go to the museum, where he shows me inscriptions in a language and script described as Sabaean, from the period before the Axumite Kingdom. We know a lot about The Axumite Kingdom. Our knowledge of Saba, before it, is growing. These inscriptions date from around 600 BC, just a few hundred years out from the Queen of Sheba.

At the Holy Trinity Cathedral, built to commemorate the victory of the Italian fascists in 1937, we look at the great marble tombs of Emperor Haile Selassie and his wife lie, decorated with his monarchical symbol, the conquering lion of the Tribe of Judah. This feels very Old Testament in all its dignity. Stained glass windows outline the narrative of the Old Testament: the Garden of Eden, Noah, Abraham, Moses and the tablets, Solomon and Sheba.

It is a tableau of kingship. Solomon, has manly stature, a full beard and long straight brown hair. His cloak is crimson. Behind him are wise men with white beards, some in Arab headdresses. Solomon extends his arm towards the Queen of Sheba on the right of the window, and she offers her hand in a formal gesture. She is wearing the traditional Ethiopian crown and ceremonial cape in red and gold, with a white and gold dress beneath.

I study her face and suggest—a little hesitantly—that she does not look very African. She has a long straight nose, a slightly Egyptian hairstyle and her skin is quite light. Tariku explains the cosmopolitan nature of his race. If she looks a little Arab, a little Asian, a little Egyptian, well all this is visible in Ethiopia. She is the Queen of Sheba, not an African queen. "So when the Queen of Sheba is claimed as Makeda by Ethiopia and Bilqis by Yemen, she could in fact be both?" He gestures at the picture.

"She is of the Red Sea. Asian. African."

We go to St George's Cathedral, built on an older church in the late nineteenth century and named after St George after the ark of this church was carried into the Battle of Adwa and victory against the Italians when the two countries were at war. The fascists set fire to it in 1937, but it was restored by Emperor Haile Selassie in 1941, who was crowned there. The painting here of Solomon and Sheba is one I had wanted to see very much. It is by Afwork Tekle, who died in 2012 who painted Mother Ethiopia and the Total Liberation of Africa.

Eyob had already shown be images of these pictures and explained why they were so significant. The Queen of Sheba becomes a symbol for African empowerment became especially potent during the reign of Emperor Haile Selassie.

Selassie was a charismatic figure, who took the story of Solomonic heritage beyond Ethiopia. Because of him, Solomon and Sheba are celebrated in Jamaica, woven into the culture of Rastafarians. The birth name of Haile Selassie was Ras Tafari. For Rastas, he is the black messiah, representing Jah—or God. The Jamaican Black Nationalist Marcus Garvey uttered a prophecy which Haile Selassie appeared to fulfil at his coronation in 1930: "Look to Africa when a black king shall be crowned, for the day of deliverance is near." In 1966, Haile

Selassie visited Jamaica, and among the rapturous crowds was the wife of a young musician called Bob Marley.

As a result and in further evidence of the many strands of religion that find their way into the Solomonic legend, this is a pilgrimage site for Rastafarians. I have a copy of the fourteenth-century *Kebra Nagast*—The Glory of Kings—edited by the American writer Gerald Hausman, with an introduction by Ziggy Marley, Bob Marley's son.

Marley writes: "This book is about the mind. It is about black history, my history, black my story."

The wisdom he retrieves from *The Kebra Nabast* is that: "Each person must go through their own tribulations until spiritual enlightenment takes place—until he sees the love of life, love of self, love of a tree, love of bird, love of bee. Everybody has to go through this."

The preface to the book sets out the claims for *The Kebra Nagast*, referring to the Queen of Sheba by her Ethiopian name, Makeda: "*The Kebra Nagast* gives us reason to believe that Makeda studied Solomon's wisdom and integrity as a ruler and brought it back to Ethiopia... What is interesting about this particular history is that it supports what certain scholars describe as the legitimate claim of blackness in biblical lore. The idea is not new. The Solomonic line, according to myth, is 'mixed' and thus black people in the Bible, as well as in Coptic literature, are, indeed, among our most famous patriarchal and matriarchal figures. Moses, for example, was said to be the husband of a Cushite woman. Makeda was certainly black."

> The Queen of Sheba: "I am black but beautiful, oh daughters of Jerusalem."
> Marcus Garvey: "Black is beautiful."
> A modern slogan is born.

To finish, we go to the National Museum to see the cast of Lucy, the 3 million-year-old skeleton discovered in the Afar district in 1974 and identified as the forerunner of the human race. In an upstairs room, there is another portrait of Solomon and Sheba—this time she is darker than he is, tall, and they are clasping hands rather than extending their arms towards handshakes. Another picture nearby catches my eye. It portrays the end first of slavery and then of colonisation in Africa. At the centre is a black woman in a long white dress, hands outstretched in joy and liberty. She stands in a natural centre stage, the spotlight of heaven upon her. It is not named as an image of the Queen of Sheba, but it has her spirit.

Tariku and I meet Eyob early next morning for the flight to Axum. We talk again about Ethiopian time and the logic of a system of counting that does not acknowledge zero but starts at one. The clocks seem to give alternative times, but I am glad to see society still runs on international time. Eyob sits next to a frail, elderly monk, who is planning to hoist himself up one of the rope lifts that control access to monasteries in Tigray. The spirit is strong here.

I am showing Eyob my pictures of Freemasons Hall, near Covent Garden, London. A wall painting of horses pulling a chariot across two columns. Above the columns is the all-seeing eye. Beneath, a shape that Eyob is uneasy about. It is the hexagon, which has a heritage from Pythagoras but is also used for black magic. Satanists insert horns into the shape. Tariku points out that it appears on the Ethiopian national flag, and that there is an is an argument going on about whether it should be removed. We move on to the safer ground, the Freemasons' attachment to the compass, and on to William Blake's great poem, God and the Compass.

After the close humidity of Addis, Axum is bright and clear. Despite his work on Ethiopian religious symbols, Eyob has never been here before and is buoyant with discovery. He thought Axum would be much bigger as a place of pilgrimage. In fact, it is a modest town. We look at the first to fourth centuries burial structure near St Mary's Church. Here is Sabaean influence, with a monolithic stone and symbolic reference to the Moon God, worshipped in Yemen and in Egypt. "It is the mathematics that interests me," says Eyob. The ancient philosophy connects Solomon to Sir Isaac Newton.

Another element that attracts the attention of Tariku, a tombstone of granite that, on its surface, bears the symbol of the Ark of the Covenant—an inner and outer square, with a triangle on top. On the underside of the monument is a swirling rose-like symbol. Tariku, competing with Eyob for ancient knowledge, points out that it is typical of the tombs of Cyrus, the Persian king, running Ethiopia in about 500 BC. We are getting nearer the time of Makeda. While so little is really known of Ethiopian archaeology, theories flourish.

The devout nature of Ethiopia is apparent from the start, a deep Christian faith, laced with older truths and legend. In 457 AD, nine Syrian saints arrived and took the gospel to many monasteries. It is still a land of monasteries. The country's highland culture has protected it against invasion. It resisted colonialism from the Italians in the late nineteenth century. It has traded rather than fought.

But religion dates from long before the Syrians arrived. It is deep and old. Homer in the Iliad talks of a human ancestor, Aithiops, who lived in the far east of known lands. He was so virtuous that he had a special relationship with the gods. Zeus paid a visit to the 'blameless Ethiopians'. Lactantius Placidus in the fifth century AD wrote that the "Ethiopians are certainly the justest men and for that reason, the gods leave their abode frequently to visit them." Solomon's wisdom was passed down.

Linguistic studies suggest that Semitic languages were first spoken in Africa then moved across the Red Sea into Arabia around 2000 BC. The Semitic speakers then migrated back to Africa a thousand years later. Followers of Mohammed, who fled in 622, after a plot against him, also arrived in Ethiopia. Mohammed says in the Koran: "Ethiopia is a country of peace! The Ethiopians are peaceful! You Arabs do not provoke Ethiopia."

The arrival of Christianity in Axum is told through another legend, involving the sea. Two Syrian boys, Frumentius and Aedesius, were on their way to India when their boat was attacked at a port of Red Sea. They were taken to the king's court at Axum. Frumentius was an evangelist and in about 342 AD he went to Alexandria, whence he returned, having been consecrated, as Bishop of Axum. He is still venerated as Abba Salama, the Father of Peace, or the Bringer of Light.

In 637 AD, the Islamic army's conquered Syria and in 639 AD Egypt, leaving the Christian church there diminished, but retaining hold over Ethiopia. Meanwhile, the Arabian navy began to dominate the Red Sea. The kingdom of Axum started to lose its maritime power.

It is not just the stones; it is the language and culture which is differently interpreted. I ask my guides if it is possible that the Sabaean language arrived here with Cyrus, from Persia. "Which version do you want? Church, history, or oral tradition?"

Either language migrated, or it emerged and was exported. Or exported only to migrate back. These days we talk about Afro-Asiatic rather than Arabian.

On the edge of Axum is a stele—a stone slab—with inscriptions from the first king to convert to Christianity in the fourth century. The inscriptions are in three languages, Greek—as spoken by the traders—Ethiopic Geez, and Sabaean, from southern Arabia, a language which gave the country its former name of Abyssinia. This civilisation is so cosmopolitan; its lines cannot be disentangled.

Its stories are fabulously woven over many years. Dominating the peaceful square is the Church of Our Lady Mary of Zion, next to the chapel which claims possession of the Ark of Covenant. There are rare historical accounts of foreigners who claim to have seen it.

An Armenian priest called Dimotheos Sapritchian, who came to Axum in 1860, described it as: "Pinkish marble of the type found ordinarily in Egypt. Quadrangular, 24 cm by 22 cm wide and only 3 cm thick. On the edges, it was surrounded by engraved flowers about half an inch wide, in the centre was a second quadrangular line in the form of fine chain... while the space between the two frames contained the Ten Commandments, five on one side, five on the other, written obliquely in the Turkish fashion."

A less prosaic account came from the coronation of Emperor Iyasu I (1682–1706).

"Then the king looked upon the Ark of Zion and spoke to it face to face... Then the Ark spoke and gave counsel to the king giving him wisdom and wise counsel to govern the earthly world and to inherit the heavenly world."

Eyob says that earlier texts of *The Kebra Nagast* give the Queen of Sheba a larger role than later ones. She is much admired in Ethiopia, but she also poses a slight problem for the conservative church. A powerful woman of pagan origins who became a single mother. No wonder some versions prefer to concentrate on her son Menelik. It may be convenient to alter the calendar of events on this occasion.

We drive on a short distance to Dungar, to the ruins that locals call the Queen of Sheba's residence, despite its history dating of the sixth century AD. The fountain of youth was very effective, for she would have been about 1,500 years old to have lived here.

The so-called Queen of Sheba's residence moved to the Axumite period in which it more properly fits, is near a mountain from which stone was quarried. It was clearly a noble's residence if not a queen's. A model of the building is in the Addis museum and it has a lovely symmetry—inner and outer squares. It is more feminine in design and less splendid than Solomon's Temple, but the setting is harmonious; cultivated fields and mountain range. The Sabaean temple at Yeha, built around 700 BC, and which we visit tomorrow, promises to be grander.

As we drive off up the mountain path towards Yeha, I notice the name of the local elementary school at Adwa. It is called the Queen of Sheba. The afternoon light is pure Old Testament Revelations as we weave our way down the mountain path. Solomonic wisdom seems to come with light and water. The day of epiphany for Ethiopia is 20 January, on which day all the Arks of the Covenant kept in every church are brought out to travel to the nearest water.

Water is creation and rebirth. Eyob cites the name of Axum itself, meaning King of Water. It hurt Ethiopia for religious and psychological reasons as well as for political ones to lose its coastline when Eritrea became independent in 1991. The opening up of the Eritrean port of Edulis for Ethiopia fills them with hope. Until now they have had to import and export through Djibouti. The Sabaean kingdom, evoked at Yeha, looks out again towards its old port on the Red Sea.

After sunset, we go to find the German archaeological team, who are excavating at Yeha and staying in a hotel down the road. Dr Iris Gerlach has just arrived to take charge and the team are talking through the day's findings over a communal table in a courtyard under the moon. They have the specialist's sense of clarity, purpose and enthusiasm. I remind Iris of her mantra when I met her last: "Let us start with what we know."

They have been on site since dawn. I sit opposite Professor Dr Norbert Nebes, of Jena University. He is of the bright face and unmodulated voice—"I know OXFORD"—and a historian of Sabaean inscription. I casually raise again whether the language is indigenous or migrated from southern Arabia and he winces at the breadth and therefore the crassness of the line of enquiry.

Naturally, I am hesitant at this stage to ask him to speculate about the Queen of Sheba, but he becomes quite giggly beneath his erudition and gives two signs of encouragement. The first is that he is dead keen on the Red Sea trade and is happy to consider the Queen as a maritime superpower.

Second, intriguingly, is a pattern of Sabaean inscriptions during the first millennium BC. They follow the maternal line. Women had status, if not as queens, then as rulers or companions. This explains some of the integration of the time. It was a trading mentality, and women may not necessarily have been spouses but could have been friends or lovers. The Queen of Sheba, a trader and a lover, is a conceivable figure. Tomorrow, at Yeha, I will have a fuller sense of how she might have lived.

Dr Norbes grows passionate in discussion with Eyob on the more solid territory of the consonant sounds of the Sabaean, language and the reading of the right to left, then left to right. The young German chef to the party confides to me: "We try not to let Dr Nebes become too excitable."

I am woken by birdsong and the pink grey light of dawn. Figures in white, people going to prayer or to trade, hurry along the wide tree and bush lined street. There is a white-flowered Cordia Africana tree outside the window. Traffic builds: tuk-tuks, donkeys and carts, bicycles, construction trucks, a few jeeps. Street sweepers clean the roads, which are already litter-free. The roundabouts are large tin drums. No plastic here, although no internet connection for me either. The wave line of the hills and jutting mountains, like great cloaks, reminds you to look up. The air is pristine. Crows are on the wing.

As we drink black coffee and eat white Ethiopian honey on toast, Eyob and Tariku throw in another strain of folklore. The question that concerns them is who was the indigenous community before the Sabaeans? Tariku has tried out his theory on Dr Nebes that they were the Agew (or Zagwe) dynasty, who prospered under the twelfth-century Christian king of Lalibela, Nakutoleab. Their lineage also included the 'Queen of the night' Queen Judith, or Gudit, who destroyed the temple at Axum. A useful monarchical oral tradition for them was their own link with Solomon and Sheba. According to Zagwe tradition, Solomon also slept with the Queen of Sheba's maid, who was of Zagwe lineage and gave their monarchs legitimacy.

In this remote and rural region of Ethiopia, the Chinese built roads are superb, although one mountain route is known locally as the Red Terror. We drive through a spectacular mountain range—some fancifully compared to the shapes of lion's heads, with citrus coloured teff fields and elaborate agricultural terraces. The climate is warm and fresh. In the Queen of Sheba's time, the climate here was a few degrees warmer and more humid. There were more rivers and springs too.

As we turn down the unmade road towards Yeha, we pass donkeys, cattle, goats and, for the first time, camels. The palace and temple of Yeha are on the edge of a village, which has led to complex compensation negotiation discussions with the Ethiopian Government. The team of Germans and Ethiopians have been working there since dawn, excavating layers from agricultural terraces down to the Sabaean foundations. Even in its ruined state, it is magnificent. We pass a giant fig tree and a fence of thorns, eucalyptus and pepper trees, aloe plants. Following a path through sweet-smelling juniper trees, we come to the sweeping staircase of what was once a five-storey, 30 × 30-metre residence, built around 800 BC. It is extremely close, given the lack of exact dating, to the time of Queen of Sheba.

This was the birthplace of the ancient Sabaean civilisation, and it is the best example of its kind, now that temples on the other side of the Red Sea at Baraqish, near Marib, are believed to have been damaged in bombing from the Saudi led coalition in Yemen's civil war.

If we wanted to make a case for the Queen of Sheba's territory crossing from Ethiopia to Yemen, Yeha is the place to do it. It has been a cosmopolitan centre between Africa, the Middle East, the Mediterranean, and the Indian Ocean, linked by the Red Sea route. The temple of Yeha was dedicated to the god Almaqah, also worshipped in Yemen.

He is called a moon god, but the image of a bull's head and a vine broadens the appeal. The Temple of Barran, six columns and a sacred well, near Marib, also called the Throne of Bilqis, is a Sabaean tribute to him. Yeha is a more ambitious construction. The building stones, measuring up to 3 metres and fitted without mortar based on exact geometry, were made of limestone, used in just the same way in the same period in Yemen.

The stones came from a quarry more than eighty miles south. The masons came from Southern Arabia, integrating with the Cushitic Agaws. The Sabaean inscriptions are the oldest available written materials in Africa, south of the Sahara. Some inscriptions show lineage, others cheering practicality. Stones are documented to give the master mason a price. There are further Sabaean details—stones that would have formed a well, and a stone tunnel to wash away the blood from animal sacrifices. An ibex stone frieze has been found, another shared bond with Yemen.

The community here is rich in ancient artefacts. One local family were using for festivities a large plate, which turned out to be a bronze age Sabaean cauldron. Pottery, dotted and decorated adds to the cosmopolitanism. The shapes are Sabaean—vase-like, but the clay is local. Furthermore, the shiny black lids are of Egyptian style. This is a trading centre.

The integration of Yemen and Tigray, just 450 miles apart, in the early first millennium is evident in the art, the architecture, the language and the writing. The Queen of Sheba belongs to both cultures. The archaeology of Yemen might be older, but the tradition of women rulers in Ethiopia is stronger. The Queen of Sheba, Judith from the Zagwe dynasty, and Queen Candace, whose Ethiopian eunuch was, according to the New Testament, the first man to baptise after the apostles. Helena, the mother of Constantine the Great, is celebrated at the Feast of the Finding of the True Cross in September. This also marks the end of the summer. St Mary is venerated above all. The Ethiopian tradition recognises Hanna, the mother of the Virgin Mary, and puts her at the heart of creation.

"And when He made an end of creating His creation, He created out father Adam... at that time Mary, the daughter of Joachim, existed in the belly of Adam in the form of white pearl which shone in his right side." Before the virgin birth, Hanna told her husband Joachim that she dreamed of a dove sitting on her head, and entering her stomach.

Ethiopian priests preach the Covenant of Mercy; those who pray to the Mother of God will be saved. The arc of women in The Bible is clear. Eve was the source of sin, Mary was redemption. The Queen of Sheba has been accused of both roles.

At Yeha, a pagan queen was absorbed into a Christian culture, at Marib into an Islamic one. Eyob points out a pagan story to explain the stone gulley to wash away the animal sacrifice. It was also the path of the serpent. Serpent worship was strong in this area. The Queen of Sheba was said to have serpent ancestry. Serpents were also jinns and dangerous.

Frankincense burned at the altar of Yeha is common to both religions and territories and we know that the Queen of Sheba (whether Makeda or Bilqis) oversaw trade in frankincense. The frankincense trail is her story. From the temple, you can look down an old road towards the port of Edulis: a farm path, dotted with cattle and women carrying grass bundles, at the start of the harvest. This could have been the caravan route to the port—gold, frankincense, ivory, obsidian, the cargo of a great sea journey to Jerusalem. It has been calculated that it would have taken nine days by donkey or camel to Edulis.

The German archaeological team have been working here since 2009, but retain their imaginative excitement. In the middle of this agricultural settlement was a fourteen metres high limestone temple and a five-storey palace. The hope is that this will become a world heritage site in 2020.

Dr Iris, coated in dust, but lustrous, emerges with maps, directions, measurements, full of facts. Eyob asks about fertility symbols and she answers smiling: "But everything is about fertility here."

Dr Gerlach, who worked in Yemen before starting work in Yeha in 2009, believes trade is the key to Saba. Here was a place that had invented metallurgy for knives and sickles, and could produce wheat and teff, a fine grain. There was more rain in Ethiopia than in Southern Arabia, which made it a good place to settle. The incense trade was at its height in Ethiopia, Yemen and Oman. There was gold and ivory. It was a charming civilisation.

The palace would have pleased a modern Arabian ruler. A reconstructed architectural drawing shows a sweeping staircase up to an entrance of six columns. It is divided into tower-like structures. As Dr Gerlach puts it: "It is the oldest skyscraper in the region." She would have expected a Yemen style courtyard in the middle of the building but cannot yet work out the source of light in the interior of Yeha palace. The spacious ground floor rooms were probably used to store trading commodities.

The roof is shaped like the steles, pyramid-shaped. It was ingeniously studded with wooden beams layered into the stone and had hardwood juniper wood flooring. This was its tragedy; a fire in about 500 BC destroyed much of the building.

Archaeologists must be patient optimists. I meet a young German on site, specialising in carbon dating of wood, who is studying the charred remains of juniper. It is so doused in protective alcohol the team say it smells like a bar. He hopes to trace the rings if he can find enough samples to corroborate. The period between 600 BC and 800 BC is apparently hard to track for carbon dating. And since the local architecture was of round huts with wooden posts, nothing has survived there to help chronology. Geologists have been luckier with evidence of rocks and water in the area. "There are still so many question marks," sighs Iris.

She is so cautious with speculation, that her hypothesis has an air of gay abandon.

One of the finds has been of the skull of a lion. "I do believe that this could be the Land of Punt. It is near the Red Sea, you have a trade of ivory and obsidian—wanted by Egypt. It makes sense that this was the centre of a trade network."

On the road back in the afternoon sunshine, Eyob is thoughtful. He says that he understands his Sabaean heritage. "Ethiopians are quite like Yemenis." Remember, Ethiopia's borders were only set in the nineteenth century, through treaties decided by the colonial powers of Europe.

Herodotus, the Greek historian, (between 400 and 300 BC) believed there were two Ethiopias, one from the South of Egypt down to the fabulously named Cinammonomorphous near India, the second further south. The Nile River has its source in Ethiopia (Lake Tana). The *Periplus of the Erythrean Sea* traced Ethiopia from Berbera to the Red Sea. In the Old Testament, 'Cush' (Hebrew) or Ethiopia (Greek) had strong relations with Arabia, Persia, Israel, Egypt and Libya.

116

It set the model for Renaissance Venice, when oriental spices, glass, astronomy and mathematics was brought in from the East to be traded with European wood, grain and leather. La Serenissima was a commercial and financial hub that also produced great art. No wonder the artist Veronese found inspiration in the notion of the Queen of Sheba arriving laden with trading treasures.

As Diodorus Siculus, a first-century BC Roman historian, said: "There is an abundance of gold and silver in Saba where the royal palace is situated. They have embossed goblets of every description, made of silver and gold, couches and tripods with silver feet, and every other furnishing of incredible costliness."

Now there is little more than metal, stone and inscriptions. Has the wealth of Saba all been lost, or is there more to discover under the ground? What crossed the Red Sea between Yemen and Ethiopia?

The journey of the stone from the quarry to Yeha is an intriguing story in itself. What kind of ancient engineering could carry stones of that size? The limestone quarry is at Wukro, eighty or so miles south. There are two ancient sites by Wukro. One is an Axumite limestone rock church, dedicated to the early Christian martyr St Kirkos, which, in the fourth century AD, is 800 years earlier than the famous churches of Lalibela. Inside, a cross is carved in the shape of the Maltese cross, later taken up by the Knight Templars. The other is the site of the Meqaber Gaewa temple, at 800 BC the same period as Yeha.

The sanctuary of Meqaber Gaewa, near Wukro, was a single podium temple with a portico and staircase. It was first excavated in 2008 by a joint German Ethiopian mission, and its altar and artefacts were taken to Wukro Museum.

The most striking of these is a limestone statue of a female figure, in a full-length decorated robe, sitting on a throne. Her head is missing; her body is balanced and confident. She is holding two scrolls and her seat is on a raised podium, which is Sabaean iconography. The inscription reads:

Almaqah [the moon god], may he grant the blessing of (male) offspring. A pagan female ruler, who gives birth to a son. Could this have been an inspiration for the Queen of Sheba, a pagan queen who needed to be converted with the advent of Judaic then Christian and then Islamic faith?

The legends and interpretations surrounding the Queen of Sheba certainly have pagan origins. The serpent heritage, the webbed feet, the curious later references to Lillith. Solomon had mastery over animals and spirits, and in some folklore, the jinns spot a rival in the Queen of Sheba, which threatens them. The

Queen of Sheba may be venerated by Jews, Christians and Muslims, but she came from Saba and Almaqah is part of her heritage.

On the front of three incense burners is a motif of the Sabaean god Almaqah, also found on stelae. Scholars say it is either a full moon and a half moon, the sun and a half-moon or half-moon and star.

There is one last thing that I stare at. It is the incense route through this region—Felix Arabia, as the Romans call it—in 70 AD, from Hadhramaut to Mecca, to Medina to Hegra to Petra to Gaza or Damascus. Saba is in sight of Ethiopia. Yemen, and what is now Oman, have cultivated incense since ancient times. But there are also incense trees in Ethiopia and Eritrea. The countries surrounding the Mediterranean, on the Nile and the Middle East, were desperate for incense. The Punt Expedition brought back incense trees, but they did not flourish in Egypt. It was the countries on the Southern Arabian peninsula that grew rich and powerful on the incense trade.

Eyob and I are finally talked out on the Queen of Sheba and sit in the back of the car in silence back to the airport. He starts to talk wistfully about an Italian restaurant in Addis. He looks at photographs on his phone of a holiday in Greece he went on with his girlfriend.

Meanwhile, I am thinking of the Claude Lorrain painting. The story is the journey. And the journey was both for a woman to meet a man and for a tradeswoman to meet a buyer. Frankincense was the Queen of Sheba's commodity. I want to find out more about frankincense and its origins. I have seen the Queen of Sheba in art and heard her in music. If I go to Dhofar in Oman, the home of frankincense I can smell her.

Chapter 10

Oman, January Following the Queen of Sheba Along the Frankincense Route

It is Christmas in Norfolk, with a north wind lashing the rain against the windows. I draw the curtains and pull my chair closer to the fire. I pick up a small pottery frame, shaped like a tiny table, take a pair of tongs and pick a small, glowing coal from the grate, placing it in the centre of the pottery frame.

The red dulls slightly, but it is still hot. I take some tweezers and reach into a small bag, half full of little yellow resin balls, each smaller than a pea. I lift one of the balls, blow the coal back into life and place the little ball carefully on top. First, I see a spiral of smoke. Then I smell the scent. It is dense and rich, so rich that it catches the back of my throat. This plain drawing room now evokes a Roman church. Frankincense: the root of the wealth of the Queen of Sheba.

The ancient Egyptians called it 'the sweat of the gods fallen to Earth'. They believed that the dead ascended to heaven on smoke produced from the smouldering frankincense. It was not just the Egyptians. The Persians, Babylonians, Assyrians, Greeks and Hebrews sought it for ceremonial use. It will not have the same value again, although demand is increasing. It has become a contemporary antidote to anxiety and there are warnings that the supply is in peril.

The Queen of Sheba's story is intimately bound with the frankincense trade. *Song of Songs* drips with gold and incense. Her kingdom was the world centre of frankincense. The precious commodity explains the trade route that she took. My supply has come by more prosaic means, brought back from a tourist store. But I know it was formed under the same Arabian sun.

Frankincense came from Dhofar, southern Arabia, in what is now Oman, and was the greatest source of wealth for the region. It was the oil and gas of antiquity. It was used—as it still is in the Orthodox and Catholic churches—for religious ceremonies and for libations. The Egyptians and the Romans were mad for it. Sheba was a frankincense paradise.

After the Christmas festivities, the family disperse and my husband I go to our favourite place, Holkham beach, just as the light is fading. We watch the pink-footed geese in skeins over the marshy land and the cry of ducks and lapwings resting in the field. It is bitterly cold and my fingers are numb, but I do not put down my binoculars. It is the spirit of migration that is so romantic and poignant. The geese come, by instinct and habit, from Siberia. And then they leave again.

I have been puzzling over why the Queen of Sheba did not stay in Jerusalem, become a wife of Solomon. And I see it is that she did not belong and that she had the freedom to leave. She did not want to be another of his conquests. She came by the frankincense route, and she returned there. I tell my husband: "I am going to Oman." He knows this is the prelude to my voyage on the Red Sea. He says to my unexpected pleasure: "Then I will come with you."

He knows that love is giving freedom but not losing sight of boundaries.

All the perfumes of Arabia came from this trading population on the Red Sea. We've ample evidence of that. Spices were an expression of the Orient. Arab dhows crossed the Indian Ocean to the Red Sea. From the ports of southern Oman, they could be transferred by caravans of camels across the empty quarter desert towards Jordan.

Or they were taken up the Red Sea to Aqaba on the Jordan Israel border and then crossing the southern desert to Jerusalem. Or onto the port of Alexandria in Egypt. I picture the spices being loaded onto boats in the busy mercantile bustle. It is the scene from the embarkation of the Queen of Sheba by Claude Lorrain.

The Roman historian Pliny was confident that Saba was the land of incense. He wrote: "There is no country in the world that produces frankincense except Arabia and indeed not the whole of that. Almost in the very centre of that region are the Atramitae, a community of the Sabaei, the capital of whose kingdom is Sabota, a place situated on a lofty mountain. At a distance of eight stations from this is the incense-bearing region known by the name of Saba." This was the place of which Heroditus the Greek historian wrote in the fifth century that "the whole country exhales a more than earthly fragrance."

This was the land known as Arabia Felix by Romans—Happy Arabia. The Red Sea in the West, the Persian Gulf in the East—and let's suggest Ethiopia in the South.

It is now called by geologists the Fertile Crescent, verdant, flourishing prosperous.

I want to follow the birds and their cinnamon leaves. But it is not enough to know where frankincense is from. I also want to know how it moved around the region. Was it all from Arabia? Or could it have come from India, too? The trade routes are still being debated.

Recent advances in organic residue carried out on small Iron Age (eleventh to tenth centuries BC) Phoenician clay flasks show that trade not only took place much earlier than previously thought but also that it covered far greater distances. Several flasks contained cinnamon. By the time of Solomon's period in the tenth century, there was a trade route in spices. The Greeks called Yemen—the Sabaean kingdom which could have included Ethiopia—the land of spices, the Chinese called it the land of the milk perfume. Imagine the possibilities of the trade!

The heart of the frankincense trade in ancient Arabia was Mirbat, now Dhofar. It is in the south of Oman, about 100 miles from the Yemen border. I look at the passenger seat map while away the Air Oman night flight from London, via Muscat, capital of Oman. I see that the Horn of Africa at Djibouti almost kisses Yemen in the Gulf of Aden. Of course, the Queen of Sheba could have united these two regions. I trace her Red Sea route up to Suez, where she would follow the fork to Al Aqaba. Then I notice that the map registers only Palestine. There is an unnamed region and no sign of a place called Israel. Some Arab countries continue to wish it out of existence. The politics of the Middle East are as fraught now as in the days of the Queen of Sheba.

I am staying at a new hotel in Salalah, the Al Baleed Resort, a sign of the country's increasing confidence in luxury travel. Oman yearns to be known only for trade and luxury, as in ancient times. Guests are welcomed with a cold towel, and a Queen of Sheba drink; ginger, frankincense, sugar syrup, rosewater. My husband and I sleep in modern luxury—a vast bed and expensive mattress, looking out into a courtyard and a private pool. The source of wealth is tourism now rather than frankincense.

The market stalls I pass on the way to the hotel are abundant with coconuts, bananas and papayas. A camel wanders up the Dubai standard wide airport road. It is the second city after Muscat, intent on progress, yet pleasantly traditional. "We are still out on our dhows," says a guide in white Arab dress. By the pool, a group of women in niqabs take selfies.

Just a few hundred yards down the beach, I come to the evidence that Salalah has known luxury before: the ruins of Sumhuram, a large port complex perhaps 2,000 years old, once an important port for the frankincense trade.

There is not much left standing—the ruins of a noble's residence, a temple and a harbour. But it is the position of it that makes my heart soar.

I stand at the sea gate, looking out at the harbour, which opens out from a lagoon. The city walls surround Sumhuram, but a passage allowed the boats to unload, and for the frankincense to be stored. It is easy to imagine the dhows, with their white sails, heading out across the sea.

It is at the heart of the trade route. Sumhuram was later documented as the port of Moscha Limen cited in the Periplus of the Erythrean Sea, in the first century AD.

The Periplus log marvels again at the divine powers attributed to the port:

"Incense can stand on the quay without being guarded thanks to the power of a god who protects it. Not even a grain of the precious resin can be loaded unlawfully. If a grain of incense is loaded the ship cannot sail for it is against the will of the god."

Were these the pagan gods worshipped by the Queen of Sheba? The moon god Al Amaqah might have held sway over it.

Much later the thirteenth-century merchant Marco Polo also recognises this port:

"This place lies near the sea and has a good port, frequented by many ships. Numbers of Arabian horses are collected here from the inland country, which the merchants buy up and carry to India, where they gain considerably by disposing of them. Frankincense is likewise produced here and purchased by the merchants.

"Frankincense helped create a maritime silk road which stretched from the Mediterranean to India and China."

We know there was a valuable trade route from the first millennium BC. From Oman—Arabia Felix—boats sailed north-east up the coast towards the Persian gulf or east to India and China. In the other direction, dhows made their way down the east coast of Africa or curled west from Oman up the Red Sea towards the Mediterranean.

The links with neighbours are further evident in the plants here. Here is the desert rose, otherwise found on the island of Socotra, off the coast of Yemen. The region of Mirbat grows the African baobab tree. But frankincense is particular to Dhofar. Different qualities of aromatic gums are found here. The white fluid which seeps from the cut bark forms the perfume of Arabia. I am going to see at last the frankincense trees, which gave the Queen of Sheba her wealth.

First, I walk around Sumharam and look out at the Arabian sea. My husband and I are alone apart from an Omani family, parents quietly teaching their children about the ancient version of their land. It is not as removed as, say Greece and ancient Athens. The lay of the land, the sea, and the routes have not changed. It feels as it is—on the tip of Arabia, with a pull towards India.

I find a reference to two first-century AD manuscripts on sea science. The first measured the stars and gave the signs of the Zodiac. The second, also familiar in the age of Periplus, is a manuscript in astronomy. It includes a description of the planets and their positions and variations in their measurements. It is illustrated with representations of constellations and of the stars that constitute them, along with measurements of latitude and longitude.

The manuscript was written by Abu Al Hasson in 986 AD. Navigators were expected to observe the colour of the water, clouds, sky colour, the scent of the land on the breeze, the swell patterns of the waves. Birds were carried on board because the direction of their flight indicated the direction of the land. Instruments were developed to measure the angles between the horizon and the sun, moon and stars. Sandglasses or hourglasses were used to measure time. Omani boats have a long history. Boatbuilders in this region were lashing planks together more than 4,000 years ago. Their tools were stone and bone and then iron and bronze.

I screw up my eyes and imagine those boats bobbing about on this glittering expanse of the Arabian sea.

The place was first excavated in 1952 by the American archaeologist and oil sheikh Wendell Phillips, known as the American Lawrence of Arabia. During this period he had won permission from the King of Yemen to excavate Marib, the claimed site of Queen of Sheba's palace. When the mission was aborted, Phillips turned his attention to Oman, accompanied by the celebrated archaeologist Frank P Albright.

British Foreign Office archives record a later quarrel as Phillips sought permission to reach Dhofar through the British run protectorate of Aden, southern Yemen. The year was 1956, the date of the Suez Crisis, in which Israel invaded Egypt, supported by France and the United Kingdom.

The British Foreign Office sought (unsuccessfully) to get the Americans onside, so wished to be friendly to the famous archaeologist. Unfortunately, local tempers frayed. An official memo reads ruefully: "Archaeologists always seem to despise each other's capabilities and fight like angry sheep while administrators in the wilds hate unrespectful foreign interlopers."

Phillips' accounts of his experiences in Felix Arabia are a compelling mix of daring-do and frustration. He first made up his mind about exploring southern Arabia on a flight in 1949. On one hand: "It is this land of sand and dust, Bedouin and jambiya, buried temple and mud palace that awaits our return to bring new life and activity."

On the other: "Portions of South Arabia are beset with political intrigues, and border disputes abound. Whole regions are forbidden and marked insecure where blood feuds rule and the rifle is king."

Phillips loved the romance of the trade routes. "I looked back over my shoulder 3,000 years and saw long trains of camels burdened with frankincense and myrrh and sometimes with gold, pearl, ivory, cinnamon, silks, tortoiseshell and lapis lazuli. They followed the single road because there was no other; to the north, the Rub al Khali or Empty Quarter offered hundreds of miles of absolute desiccation; to the south, the barren plateau spread only a short distance before it plunged precipitously into the sea...

"Here strange vessels with huge sails swept in on the breast of the seasonal monsoons—whose variations were an oriental secret for thousands of years... At the western corner, other harbours received goods from the nearby Horn of Africa and sent them north to join the main road, which was worn deep by the flow of southern Arabian's priceless natural product—incense from the valley of the Hadhramaut and from Dhofar, the frankincense country."

His adventures, recorded in his book *Qataban and Sheba*, end with him and his party, including a fabulously glamorous translator, Eileen Salama, escaping at dawn from Yemen, avoiding a plot to murder them. The excavations of the temple at Marib are fraught with trouble.

One cable reads: "Yemeni worker knocked aside pillar support at Temple causing chain reaction six pillars fell STOP our Egyptian foreman Rais Gilani almost killed STOP Governor Marib blames Dr Jamme for incident although Jamme miles away.... All Archaeological specimens taken from Dr Albright and locked up governor holds key STOP Soldiers constantly stealing food articles from expedition headquarters STOP Please come urgently fear situation getting out of hand."

Phillips' misfortunes did not last. He had a brief encounter with the vice president of the Shell Oil Company and "at the end of my allotted time I rushed out soon to be richer by 50,000 gallons of petrol."

It may be thwarted archaeology or wistful entrepreneurism which named the ruined citadel of Sumharam as the Queen of Sheba's Palace in the literature of the place, even though excavated objects go back only so far the third century BC and even that level of antiquity has been disputed. The modern guide notes stiffly: "The kingdom of Saba was the most renowned of south Arabian kingdoms thanks to its mythical queen mentioned in both the Bible and the Koran." Mythical now, is she?

Whoever ruled Sumhuram; there were high born women here. Archaeologists have found mirrors, rods for applying kohl, bracelets, necklaces and earrings. Women from this district have ancestral knowledge of making cosmetics. Kohl, used to darken the inner rims of eyes, is derived from sources including burned shark liver and coconut, but mostly from the resinous soot of frankincense. This can be mixed with oyster shells and mother-of-pearl giving fragrance and glitter.

Since one of the Queen of Sheba's riddles to Solomon was about kohl, we can assume she used it.

I think of my own journey so far. I have delved back into my own first love and laid ghosts to rest. I look at my husband in his familiar crumpled linen shirt and shorts, binoculars poised, hoping for bird sightings. We are both on the lookout for the hoopoe bird. I think, of a platitude which is nevertheless profound. Life works out for the best. My first husband was charismatic but he was hectic. He thrived on drama. It was stable and peaceful to bring my children up elsewhere in London and in Norfolk. The entrance of the Queen of Sheba is a dazzling thing but I am hoping that life after Solomon was where her happiness lay.

I take a deep breath of heat and ocean and a whisper of frankincense. Boswellia Sacra, the tree from which the best quality of frankincense is derived, is from near here. I long to feel the glue on my finger as the Queen of Sheba once did.

There are four kinds of frankincense here.
The first is Al Hojaris, from Wadi Hojar, east of Dhofar.
The second grows in the northern slopes of the Dhofar Mountains.

The third comes from the Ashazri region, in the west.

The fourth from the southern slopes.

Now it is time to find some.

We head out to Ubar, the 'lost desert city' evoked in the *One Thousand and One Nights*, excavated by the American archaeologist and film-maker, Nicholas Clapp, author of an elegant work on the Queen of Sheba.

Clapp is a desert guy, and he traced the Queen of Sheba's plausible journey across the desert. Ubar, the ruined city fort, covered by sand, is the camel station before crossing Rub-Al Khali, the Empty Quarter. Ahead is Saudi, south is Yemen. The camels, loaded up with frankincense, set off on their desert journey. There are still the distinctive black camels, although most of their Bedouin owners are now in houses rather than tents, and tourist adventurers in four-by-four land cruisers speed through the stony desert, the flat desert and finally the caramel coloured, wind-whipped dunes.

The desert trees here are full of milk, but it is poisonous. The sand rolls and races down invisible lanes. The light and emptiness are desired by tourist adventurers to Oman, many of whom seem to toss their plastic bottles out of their cars.

The Queen of Sheba could have crossed the desert, I believe that she sailed up the Red Sea; both Axum and Southern Arabia have historically been maritime powers and Egypt is known for its sailors. It would have been quicker and grander, especially in the summer months, to be back in time for the Saba September festival. Having gazed out at the Arabian sea, it makes sense to me. The sea as a literal route and as a metaphor. The sea as the beginning of creation. The embarkation of the Queen of Sheba.

If I can first find the frankincense I reckon that I have completed all my preparations: I am ready to embark on my Red Sea journey.

We drive to a wadi, back towards Salalah, on the plateau atop the hills that rise so steeply from the coast. This is frankincense territory, a stony, semi-desert region with occasional floods. In the first millennium, there were thousands of trees in this district. In modern times, they are sparse. The land is overgrazed by camels, and the land is dryer. Furthermore, frankincense has lost its high value.

It is exhilarating to see the trees in the wild, gnarled, and rather stunted, with long, rubbery green leaves, ten to a stalk. The soft, honey-coloured bark curls easily. Our guide takes a penknife and cuts a quick wound, an orange-red under the skin, beneath the first layer of green. After a few seconds, the tree oozes small

126

drops of sticky white resin. It is gluey to the touch, and when I smell my sticky fingers, I recognise the aroma of the high church altar. I feel in touching distance of the Queen of Sheba.

In this heat, the gum resin will quickly dry to a crystal. The crystals are ready for transporting and for burning. The trees heal.

It has been an exhilarating morning and we are hungry. We stop at a roadside restaurant and I tip water over my fingers, still sticky with residue. We sit cross-legged on cushions, among other groups of men who nod at us. They are eating from bowls with their hands and wiping them afterwards with cloths. The fatty meat they are chewing is a camel. The smell of grilled camel meat from the outside fire fills my nostrils, displacing the frankincense.

Plates of meat and salad and vegetables and flatbreads are brought to our table. Suddenly we are ravenous for the greasy meat. I search in my pocket for the fluttery softness of the sliver of bark I took as a souvenir. A small desert tree, a resin on which to build a kingdom.

Much later, at the end of my journey, in the markets of Jerusalem, I shall see and smell the spices again as the Old City stirs for another day. As the shutters open in the trading streets, an outcome the bowls of spices and fruits. Myrrh, saffron, patchouli, amber, and little rocks of frankincense. I turn up the Via Dolorosa; the narrow street marking the final Stations of the Cross that Jesus is believed to have carried from Calvary to Golgotha.

I walk through the little Coptic Church that leads to the Holy Sepulchre and into an atmosphere that is thick with the cloying scent. The Magi, including the Ethiopian king, brought gifts of gold, myrrh and frankincense to celebrate Christ's birth. Here I smell the last of those at this place of his execution.

Now it is time for my voyage to begin. My ship, HMS Dragon is sailing through the Strait of Hormuz and shall be arriving at the port of Salalah in Southern Oman in time to pick me up. At last, I am going to sail up the Red Sea 3,000 years after the Queen of Sheba.

Chapter 11
The Red Sea, February A Voyage up the Red Sea, in Search of the Queen of Sheba

And when the queen of Sheba heard of the fame of Solomon concerning the name of the LORD, she came to prove him with hard questions.

"And she came to Jerusalem with a very great train, with camels that bare spices, and very much gold, and precious stones."

The Queen of Sheba's preparations were a military undertaking. I imagine the heavy caskets being loaded at the harbour, the inventories, the entourage, the provisions for the journey.

Mine was not a queenly approach. I took my instructions from a naval sheet: soft-soled shoes for the boat, passport, blood type.

I added to that some hard-wearing trousers, t-shirts a waterproof jacket, and a notebook for hard questions. I abandoned skirts because of scrambling up and down ladders all day. But I did pick a favourite silk navy dress in case of dinner with the captain. The Queen of Sheba would have thought about sea conditions, local threats, transport logistics. I am doing the same.

Oman is surrounded by sea from the Arabian/Persian Gulf, to the Arabian Sea. The Queen of Sheba travelled by dhow and camel. I came by plane and am to be a passenger on of the latest warships.

Yet travel is not guaranteed, despite all our technology. Our internal flight from Muscat to Salalah was grounded—along with most of the world's Boeing 737s—following initial inquiries into a deadly crash in Ethiopia.

And HMS Dragon is 'on task' again, so is running late. Unlike the Queen of Sheba, I am getting regular email updates, from a Ministry of Defence 'minder' who has been sent along to keep an eye on us. Now there is a worrying lull.

Nick, our minder, goes a bit quiet on me, then asks for a 'catch up' the following day. There is geopolitics going on. The tense relationship between

America and Iran is affecting the price of oil and passage of vessels through the Straits of Hormuz between the Persian Gulf and the Gulf of Oman.

There is also a frostiness between Egypt and the BBC after a report that irritated the Government. The navy is worried about dropping us off at Port Said, from where I was going to make my way to Cairo.

I may have the blessing of the First Sea Lord, but this will not necessarily filter down to the Egyptian official stamping my entry card. "And the little bit of England that can protect you will be sailing off towards the Med," says Nick.

The alternative proposal is that I stay on through the Suez Canal, cruise up the west coast of Israel and hop off in Beirut.

And yet I am determined to go to Egypt. It runs through the story of the Queen of Sheba. The magic, the serpent mythology, the language of the Song of Song, the facial features. The expedition was sent by the Pharaoh Hatshepsut down the Red Sea to Punt. I make my own private plans for getting there.

Now, finally, I am standing on a quay in Salalah. This is at last is the Claude Lorrain moment. This is the embarkation.

Before me is the elegant, pale grey, deadly shape of HMS Dragon, a British Royal Navy Type 45 Destroyer pulling into the harbour. Dragon is heading for the Red Sea, through the Suez Canal and into the Mediterranean and I am hitching a lift on her. Her: ships take the female pronoun; feminine might.

It takes half an hour to manoeuvre the ship so that it is neatly lined up at the dock. I am contentedly watching it in this hub of trading activity. It is the enaction of the Claude Lorrain painting, right before my eyes.

Salalah in ancient times was at the heart of the commercial world. It believes it can be so again. The port here is modelled on Rotterdam, in Holland, with big, open, efficient wharves designed to handle container traffic. It aims to be a regional rival to Dubai, to the north of Oman and to Djibouti, across the Gulf of Aden on the Horn of Africa, where Chinese engineers are working on a new port.

This region is of strategic importance to the great powers, now as it was 3,000 years ago. Convoys of construction lorries, piled with bags of cement, move up and down the harbour road. Hundreds of workmen in hard hats, many of them labourers brought in from India, are toiling in the heat.

This is what globalisation looks like; vast commercial ships piled high with 20-foot and 40-foot containers. When containers were standardised in the second half of the last century, they changed the world. Cargo moved more easily, lifted on cranes designed for the job, into trains and lorries and planes fitted to transport them. Ships became colossal. Around us are 200,000-ton vessels piled high with containers. The Queen of Sheba watched sacks of spices loaded on the backs of men. This is the new expression of a system of trade that has moved from a regional to a global basis.

HMS Dragon is slender and compact. Not all countries give their ships the feminine pronoun—Italy, among others, uses the male pronoun—but to me, HMS Dragon is already emphatically female—as sleek as a piece of Apple technology, its weaponry discreet. The Wildcat helicopter is out of sight, the Phalanx missile looks innocuous. The ship is here on peaceful patrol, but I soon learn that it operates with a forceful motto: "We fight tonight."

As the sun sets and the evening cools a little, a couple of tugboats fuss at the bows to guide us away from the quay. The captain, Mike Carter Quinn, invites me to the bridge, where he supervises our departure with the navigator, the quartermaster, look-outs and warfare officers.

He stands in front of banks of computers and global positioning devices but explains that, visually, things are not so very different from the Queen of Sheba's day. Modern-day sailors operate in the way of their ancestors: they calculate winds and tides, understand how to chart a course using trigonometry, look out for landmarks and for dangers: vessels in their path, reefs, pirates. Essentially, the relationship with the ocean has barely changed. Under the stars, in the open sea, says the commander, you experience 'a wonderful feeling of insignificance'.

As a sometime altar boy, he is familiar with the 'bells and smells' of the Catholic church. The first time he smelt incensed its strength—combined with his anxiety at doing the right thing in his ceremonial role—made him pass out. He is curious about the frankincense trade. There is not much moving up the Red Sea these days. Oil and gas have become the successor to frankincense.

As we move off the Oman coast we see the lights of big commercial vessels and smaller dhows, typically used for fishing in the region. Dragon is making her way back to Portsmouth, in the UK, but is looking for narcotics along the way. In the evening, the Wildcat helicopter takes off on patrol. Just before I joined Dragon, the ship's crew had seized around a quarter of a ton of heroin from a dhow carrying an Iranian flag and no paperwork. The drugs are confiscated—and destroyed—the crews released.

A crew member explains the giveaway signs—too many people on board, fresh paint, false bulkheads on. Sometimes they ask crews to prove they are fishermen by casting their nets. The drugs come down from Afghanistan and Pakistan via the Arabian Sea to East Africa and then on to Europe. The route along the Makran Coast, running on the edge of Pakistan and Iran, is known as the Hash Highway or the Smack Track. Britain is a huge market. Never mind gold from Arabia and spices from Saba, the money is now in heroin and hashish. Problems have been exacerbated by the civil war in Yemen, which is encouraging lawlessness at sea. Drugs also help pay for weapons.

The next morning, we get our first glimpse of the action. The Wildcat helicopter patrol the previous night had responded to the intelligence of a suspicious dhow sailing south and, flying almost as far from the ship as its fuel would allow, identified a suspicious dhow, blue and yellow, flying no national flag. While some of us slept, the captain had decided to take it was worth taking a 130-mile detour on a radar ping and a hunch.

Now the dhow is about five miles away and the Wildcat is preparing to take a further look. Intelligence from the helicopter matters, but someone is going to have to look the master of this dhow in the eye to get to the truth. The Wildcat will provide air cover to the two inflatable sea boats now speeding towards it. The first carries the green team of Royal Marines, armed with automatic weapons. The blue team is mixed Marines and Navy crew marines and navy, tasked with searching the boat. If the dhow crew produce weapons, the Marines are ready.

We watch the action from Dragon's bridge, which—given the absence of portholes elsewhere on the ship—feels like some kind of naval penthouse, carpeted, panoramic views, blazing daylight, horizon. The navigator, Jenny, studies the dhow through binoculars. The officer of the watch, Holly—at 21, the youngest officer on the ship—relays information.

A Farsi translator among the Marine boarding team hears the sorry story of the master of the vessel. They are an Iranian crew, innocently fishing. They have a rudder problem, which is why they are not fishing at the moment. They have no paperwork. Permission is rapidly given to board the boat. The vessel is stateless and we are in international waters, so this is not a contentious order.

The dhow is low in the water and the navy team finds out why. In the space for the nets and the ice hold, they find stacks of 20 Kg bags of hashish. One of the sea boats returns laden with the sacks: crew form a human chain to pass them up and lay them out in front of the helicopter pad. Rock music plays on the ship radio. This is the crew's eighth successful boarding and they have been making a habit of showing off their drug seizures on social media by arranging the contraband into various images. Today they have enough sacks to attempt an anchor design.

Within the 20 Kg bags are individual 1 Kg bags of hash resin. The ones I am shown are packaged up as fair trade coffee. The crew has previously found them with the names of UK high street brands faked on the bags. Each 1 Kg bag has a street value of about £3,000.

That gives the fifty bags in this haul a street value of more than £3.2 million. By the end of the day, the crew have lifted a further seventy-five of these 20 Kg bags of hashish, the last store stowed by the engine itself. More than £8 million worth of drugs. Tomorrow it will be thrown overboard. Heroin is even more valuable. As the crew tipped the proceeds of their last drugs bust overboard, one sailor looked at the £250,000 worth of heroin in one bag and said ruefully: "There goes my house."

The crew give me a ride out to the dhow in one of the bucking sea boats, a kind of berserk adventure park ride in which I hold on to the rail for dear life, across the short expanse of sea. The marines and naval team—powerful, confident, kitted up—have taken charge of the dhow. A couple of them are sitting dangling their feet over the side.

The dhow crew is huddled in the bow, among the ropes. Their boat is hot and squalid. They look thin and tired. These grey-bearded men have sailed around 700 miles and now watch their earnings disappear, so close to delivery in Yemen. They carried their own supplies of opium, so maybe users as well as dealers. For some, it is a profession, for others a way to make more money. Some fishermen also carry drugs. They are worth more than tuna, after all.

At best, they have now lost their money. At worst, they will have to explain the loss of the cargo to a dealer who suspects they have made a private sale. The navy crew feels almost sorry for them. One sighs that their stories are so pitiable. Couldn't they at least make a pretence of fishing?

Our boat bucks, pretty much vertically, back to what really does feel like the mother ship, reassuringly close to us. Commander Carter Quinn hopes drug busts like these can damage the economics of the drugs trade. Drug busting is not the principal purpose of HMS Dragon, but he believes it aids peace and security. The UK is the biggest drugs market in Europe. The traffic funds crime, terrorism and chaos. Just what Yemen could do without.

By sunset, the drugs haul is caged on the ship, ready to be tossed into the sea. Tomorrow I shall watch the ship's crew gather on the flight deck, rip open the bags, tear apart the dung-like resin, growing sticky in the heat, and lob it off the stern. Rock music will play again, and the clear sea air has the passing scent of sweet-sharp hashish. Millions of pounds worth of biodegradable, illegal drugs will drop into the water, like resin from heaven. I wonder how the tuna will feel.

But this evening it is quiet, and I go up to watch the sunset from the bridge, careful not to shut the heavy doors to prevent them rebounding, and the galley outside, being careful to open and shut the heavy doors to stop them rebounding on you, just as I have learned to go nimbly up and down ladders though still facing backwards.

The sea is so calm that I can see the violet clouds reflected in the water. Shoals of tuna are jumping at the side of the boat. There is not another vessel to be seen. The officer of the watch says that if you fully wish to know the conditions of the sea, you need to be at railing height on the bow. The Queen of Sheba would have seen the water close and felt its changing moods more acutely. This sea passage can be a lot rougher than it is today.

I look at the shipping routes on a screen as we approach the Gulf of Aden. If the sea and sky—even the broad landmass of the coast—would look the same to our traveller 3,000 years ago, navigation has moved on. Today we power down the centre of the channel, having no need of the coastal landmarks used by boats that once needed to hug the shore.

The officer of the watch shows me how perilous this could be on the Ethiopian Eritrean coast. We are safely in the area shaded black. Blue means a depth of 5—10 metres, green marks sandbanks and mudflats. There are plenty of those around Eritrea. It is also an area of piracy, then and now. If the drugs are coming from the north, the pirates are coming from the South—mostly Somalia.

This passage is too important as a trade route to allow the pirates to prey on ships. The sea has looked empty until now, but it will become busier with merchant's vessels. There will be dhows too, not all of them engaged in the innocent activity. The international community is cracking down. The Queen of Sheba did not have the international community to turn to for help, but she had her own army and singular authority.

The captain gives me a crash course in dhow recognition. The jelibuts are the basic models we have seen today. The boom cargo dhows are bigger and longer. The beautiful models are the slipper dhows, curved and slender. The Sultan of Oman has one. I wonder if the Queen of Sheba had one like it.

The ship sails on under the stars the Queen of Sheba knew. From the bridge, I look out at the calm and empty sea, the nearest vessel about sixty miles away.

Out on the bridge wing in the outside air, I look at the brightness of the moonlight picking up the luminescence of the water.

Commander Carter Quinn understands the passing of history and the cameo role of Britain from his place on the bridge. He is looking at the same scene as Admiral Nelson, as Sir Francis Drake and, yes, as the Queen of Sheba. He points up at Venus, a planet that unites sailors. In the eighteenth century, Captain James Cook set off on a voyage to Tahiti to observe the transit of Venus, which would allow an accurate measurement of the distance between the earth and the sun. On the way, he charted Pacific islands and circumnavigated the North and South islands of New Zealand and the East Coast of Australia.

The exhilarating thing is still the dark sense of the unknown, of what lies beyond the horizon. It gives him a sense of tranquillity, the vastness and depth of space, the silence of the ocean. He loves the sea and fears it. Here, in spring, it is placid. But the Atlantic can be violent. It can claim ships. Sailors dread being lost at sea.

I remember Dr Willis, the Dean of Canterbury Cathedral reflecting on the religious significance of the sea. The Sea of Galilee, Solomon's ship, the Red Sea. And, right at the start of everything, Genesis:

> In the beginning, God created heaven and earth.
> And the earth was without form and void, and darkness was upon the face of the deep. And the Spirit of God moved upon the face of the waters.
> And God said, Let there be light:
> And there was light.
> And God saw that light that it was good: and God divided the light from the darkness.
> And God called the light Day and the darkness he called Night. And the evening and the morning were the first day.
> And God said, Let there be a firmament in the midst of the waters, and let it divide the waters from the waters.
> And God made the firmament and divided the waters which were under the firmament from the waters which were above the firmament: and it was so.

On the wing of the bridge at night, you have a sense of the meaning of Creation.

The sun is up and I am back on the Bridge. Holly is Officer of the Watch. We are fifty-four miles off the coast of Yemen, to starboard—on the port side we are approaching the Horn of Africa, Somalia and Djibouti. This means we are entering China watch, the owners of Djibouti port. HMS Dragon intends to mind its own business through this stretch. In the past, the British frigates have helped escort American ships through along this Gulf of Aden. Now the Americans have turned their attention to South East Asia, tensions have moved to the international waters of the South China Sea and the Chinese are hostile to US or British presence there.

Beyond some superpower bristling, it is in everyone's interests to keep these waters open. This is the route to Suez, the great trade route of the world, used by the world, Europe, America, Russia, and China. Before Suez, this opened in 1869, which trade had to go around the Horn of Africa, expensive on time and fuel and treacherous conditions. In the captain's words: "The Suez Canal changed the world."

At its north end, the Red Sea has an arm to the west—the Gulf of Suez—and an arm to the right—the Gulf of Aqaba. Dragon is heading for Suez. The Queen would have sailed up the Gulf of Aqaba, before continuing her journey overland.

We are now approaching Aden, a port with a rich commercial history. In the seventeenth century, when the East India Company established itself, these waters became deeply desirable. A British stake in the port was gained in 1837 when a merchant ship sailing under a British flag was attacked on the Arabian Peninsula by villagers. The British sought Aden in compensation. Out of a firefight was created Queen Victoria's first colony.

The opening of the Suez Canal in 1869 gave the settlement a further strategic significance, watched closely by the Ottoman Empire. When the First World War broke out in 1914, Aden became a military settlement for the British, a pivotal base between India and Europe. It remained a key British outpost for another fifty-three years of argument, political intrigue and contentious map-making in an area of close interest to Britain, Egypt and Russia. In 1935, the Royal Navy established a base in Aden, renaming HMS Norfolk III as HMS Sheba.

No British warships have gone to Aden since the attack on USS Cole in 2002, when suicide bombers rammed a small boat into the American destroyer, killing seventeen crew. We pass through the Gulf of Aden cautiously. Last year Yemeni rebels attacked a Saudi mine hunter boat with a suicide boat. We will be on red alert for waterborne IEDs, and I improvised explosive devices. A Japanese aircraft is in sight, and signals in. It is on a counter-piracy mission.

We spot a cargo dhow en route between Somalia and Yemen, which slightly changes course when it spots us. We go to have a closer look. If it is carrying charcoal, we can intervene. Charcoal, used for shisha pipes, is also smuggled from northern Somalia in a trade that is known to fund the terrorist organisation Al-Shabab. Worse, it could be human trafficking, an activity in which this warship is not equipped to intervene, for there is nowhere any victims of the trade can safely be looked after onboard. In this case, all seems well and we are given intelligence that this is a normal trade route. The crew on the bridge relaxes.

I go out onto the bridge wing and watch the sun cast a path of light across the water in front of us, directing us to Bab el Mandeb, the strait between Yemen and the Horn of Africa, and beyond to the foot of Suez. This is what Claude Lorrain painted, an irresistible glittering path, a voyage of discovery.

Maybe not so very much has changed in 3,000 years. I stand on the bridge deck watching the acrobatics of the flying fish and the dolphins playing by the boat until the sun descending beneath the horizon turns the sky lilac. A rising full moon casts its pale light over the water. Then I see the answering colours. The churning water at the side of the boat is producing strands of gold. The sea is woven with gold. Would the Queen of Sheba in her slipper dhow have watched the water reflect her magnificent wealth back at her?

I am joined on deck by some muscular forearms against the railing and a red-tipped cigarette. I identify them as belonging to the first marine to board the drug dhow. It is his job to be 'first up the ladder'. He joined the marines having walked into the jobcentre and asked for the hardest thing they could give him. He says the main quality needed for the job is common sense. Or to put it another way: "Don't be a dick."

He makes his own judgements. In the marines' room, they were told that the Queen of Sheba was on board. Most were too polite to question the passenger list, but First-up-the-ladder Marine challenged it. "I said, I know I am stupid, but I don't think the Queen of Sheba exists."

"Well, she does now," I say.

He laughs, throws his cigarette butt overboard and shakes my hand: "Goodnight, Queen."

We are still 400 miles from Bab el Mandeb and the sea is empty but the ship's horn sounds. This is the day when the crew step up to an amber state—State 2—of readiness, and conduct tests for fire and flood as well as attack. They rehearse, for instance, eating their three-course lunch in seven minutes, known as the mess-in. the Queen of Sheba would have eaten in a more leisurely fashion.

I look in at the sickbay where the kit is being examined and made ready. The medic tells me, in the spirit of Sheba, that the stretchers, which must be able to get up the ladders on board, are of an 'ancient' design. Bamboo, cloth and rope. Modernity cannot improve on them.

I learn the meaning of horn blasts. Two short blasts for turning to port, one blast for starboard. If you are entering a crowded port, full of large and small vessels, five short blasts should clear a path. Six short blasts are the dangerous ones. That is a man overboard.

In a relaxed state, State 3, watches are four hours. In State 2, they move up to 6 hours, rotating half the crew. In State 1, everyone is on full alert. Weapons and sensors are manned and ready for use, the air search radar seeking out signals. In front of the bridge on the bow are the trap doors that will release missiles straight up into the air, if the captain orders it. Officers have changed into white overalls for the high state of readiness, giving a slightly eerie appearance to the bridge. The threats to the Queen of Sheba might have come from Nubia, Egypt, and Assyria. These days they come from the land of Sheba itself. Yemen.

I have established a pattern of standing on the bridge wing each afternoon between 4:30 and 6:30. Here is the Claude Lorrain wide, sparkling path of light in front of the ship to the horizon ahead. I am becoming used to the way the horizon circles the ship. The swell of the waves is like the ocean breathing.

Then the path of light narrows to a mellow road, but the sun becomes clearer, denser, and breathtakingly orange. The Queen of Sheba must have felt overpowered by its strength. The firmament yields to it. For her to have given up her worship of the sun so readily for Solomon shows the power of his persuasion.

As the sun dips, and the cloak of pink, red, hyacinth, spreads across the horizon I look at the early evening shapes of the loaded guns, and the tubes and balls of the chaff ready for the morning. A sign on the deck below reads: "Danger, loaded rounds may fire without warning."

I take a final look at the horizon and see what I had first thought was a grey cloud is in fact a huge vessel just off the coast of Aden. I report back to the bridge. They have not only seen it but can tell me every detail about its contents and direction. It is a container ship heading for Salalah. Every ship over 450 tonnes has to declare itself. Warships do not. The officer on the bridge says dryly that it will have worked out that we are either a warship or a dhow. A list of warships in the area is pinned up, so we know what to expect. And so we move on towards Bab el Mandeb.

It is 5:00 a.m., and I scramble up the ladder to the bridge. The great dusty moon is now in front of us—fast-moving purple clouds pass across it. The wind has picked up as we move towards the funnel of the Bab El—Mandeb straits; we are also moving faster at twenty knots through this passage. The white waves show the sea is rougher. The sight of sea birds shows there is land nearby.

On the Bridge wing with me is Helen Taylor, a warfare officer. She calmly takes me through planned procedures. If an unidentified vessel or aircraft should come towards us, Dragon might fire a flare, or give its five questioning blasts of the horn. The men wearing green will man the guns, and warning shots could be fired. The operations room would identify and classify the treat. If an attack is underway, Dragon may use the Phalanx—a close-quarters weapon for use against anti-ship missiles and helicopters—and the Oerlikon 30 mm cannon. "It is a wall of lead," says Helen Taylor.

The Captain reflects that the state of alert has been there right through maritime history. In Master and Commander, the great Patrick O Brien sea novel, the drummer 'beats the quarters' to get everyone on the station. The Queen of Sheba too would have had those on watch aboard her dhow. Whether it is out of politeness to a guest or a real sense of place, I am pleased that so many around me are now beginning to channel the spirit of the Queen of Sheba: "The rowers would have known to defend the Queen from bandits and pirates and other dangers," says the captain.

We watch the sky behind the boat change colour, the darkness overlaid with a painter's palette. It is sunrise. Helen Taylor, who has studied astro navigation, can give me the precise timings of the sunrise, altering them as we head further west. The captain learned them from the Nautical Almanac and Norie's Nautical Tables. Now it is left to a computer. As we see decipher the first grey curves of Yemen—our first sighting of land for days—Helen points up the departing stars. There is Venus, the brightest: You see it doesn't twinkle. It is a planet. Only twinkle. Then there is her favourite Scorpio, most visible in this region.

I smile in the darkness. I am looking at the Queen of Sheba's stars. Three thousand years are a blink in our universe.

The sun is up now, as we pass into Bab el Mandeb straits. On one side the landmass of Eritrea, on the other the south-west tip of Yemen. The captain lends me his binoculars and I can see clearly now the lighthouse and little houses of Mayyun Island. He looks out at the rougher waves against the rocky coast and says that it could be the north-west of Scotland. Behind us, what were spots of lights in the darkness turned out to be 200,000 tons, a Danish container ship that is almost 400 metres long? By comparison, our warship is 8,000 tons. We start to see more steel leviathans, the trade of Suez, the goods of the world.

The clear land of Yemen starts to recede. We are now into the Red Sea.

What alerts the team on the bridge now, as it would have done 3,000 years ago, is unfamiliar. There is a pattern of life at sea. In the rough waters of Bab El Mandeb, you would have been surprised, for instance, to see fishing vessels. Now we are heading north-west through the Red Sea between Sudan and Saudi, and there is a gaiety to the place. Groups of cormorants skim the water; a dolphin chases the side of the ship. Another enormous container ship passes.

Then I am called back in from the bridge wing. The second in command is checking out an anchored cargo vessel that does not fit the pattern of life at sea. More officers appear on the bridge, four of them picking up binoculars. The conversation moves between easy banter; they recently picked up on Channel 16, the internationally shared maritime channel, a captain discussing in full his tax arrangements; they discuss the consumption of the final Christmas hoard from their lockers; they remember when the ship shop closed, creating an immediate internal black market in cigarettes; then the banter is replaced by a concentrated silence. What IS that vessel? After further investigation, the ship is identified. All is well.

It is getting hard to keep track of the days. The crew said they remember them by the menu—curry Wednesday, fish Friday, steak Saturday, served and eaten briskly.

In the end, time reverts to the height of the sun and its effect on the water. I watch it starboard at 8:00 a.m., creating a lake of light through the haze over the choppy waters. The wind is stronger here, as we travel at fifteen knots towards Egypt, leaving behind Sudan. On the other side of the sea is Saudi.

It is time to test the guns, particularly the Phalanx. The mist of bullets shot at speed will take out air missiles or approaching boats. "If it flies it dies," says Tom the warfare officer, watching with his binoculars around his neck. The ship is in international weapons testing waters but is keeping an eye on the container vessel on the horizon.

Phalanx will not be deliberately fired unless we have entered a red zone, in which case it can fire automatically. A red zone? "It means when everything has gone to shit," explains Tom. "If all else fails it aims to put so much metal into incoming that it will explode." The Queen of Sheba would have relied on obsidian stone-carved weapons and hand to hand fighting.

The order comes from the bridge: 'Heads to port' and we duck. Mounting correct. Commander approved. Shoot. A cloud of bullets and a sound rather like a giant's furniture being dragged across the ceiling. "It is like a big fart," says one of the crew. A deadly one This was a 150 rounds-a-minute burst. It can be increased to 500 rounds and in extreme 4,000 rounds a minute. Phalanx shot. Phalanx relax. A lucky dolphin passes the boat, adorably unaware.

The officer looks at the 4.5-inch naval gun. He says that one really is worth watching. "When that one is fired, it shakes out the light fittings in the gunnery room."

The Queen of Sheba came in peace down the Red Sea, but, says Tom, the principles of the route are the same. The sea conditions in the Middle East are unchanged. Both the Queen's slipper dhow and HMS Dragon experience the haze and the humidity of this stretch of the Red Sea. Both navigate port side (left) and starboard. Some sailors on this ship have port side and starboard tattoos it is so much part of their existence.

The ship continues to keep a watch on other vessels, and it is a day for the team to photograph. Scott, who has the face of a Second World War pilot, sandy-haired and square-jawed, takes me up in the Wildcat helicopter to get a bird's eye view.

We wave down at the ship's crew, who have gathered in formation at the front of the bow, arms folded. There is another row on the bridge deck. The marines stand apart. We hover in sight of a tanker that has not registered on the automatic information service for ships over 300 tons. The pilots can identify type, speed, and direction. Before we return, the pilots demonstrate a nose over and a wingover, dropping dramatically, to convert height into speed. The washing machine effect is exhilarating.

Perhaps I have become institutionalised, but I am moved to see the ship at distance, just as I felt a pull towards it seeing it from the sea boat. "We are going back to mum now," says the co-pilot, and HMS Dragon does indeed feel like a maternal figure. A feminine presence is moving assuredly up the Red Sea towards Sinai, now as it was then.

Back on board, the pilots show me on their thick, green, nuclear attack proof laptop, their thermal and infrared imagery of vessels they track. Then Scott opens another folder: It is called moon and dolphins. Their equipment may be aimed at long-range targeting of hostile vessels, but at that distance, dolphins can look awfully like dhows. The camera picks up little splashes in the water, everywhere.

It goes in closer and there are shots in the Arabian Sea of hundreds of dolphins, in full acrobatics.

"Where there are dhows there are dolphins," says the pilot. "They are the policemen of the sea." As for the moon, you can see the craters up close.

It is both accessible and mysterious. It is as the Queen of Sheba would have known it.

It is a clear evening, and more importantly a clear horizon. I watch the sun fall over Ethiopia, balancing on the horizon and dropping amid a final curtsey of red gold and pink sky. The Wildcat helicopter flies past in the final moments, producing a cascade of flares from each side. The reason for the Red Sea show is a practical one. The flares will be out of date by the time the ship returns to Portsmouth, so they might as well be let off in style. The sea boats have sped to the front of the bow to watch, through smacking inky waves.

That evening, I learn how to navigate by the stars. A youthful sub-lieutenant, Ashley Purchase, has his sexton to show me and his own calculations. We go out onto the bridge wing. He identifies Sirius, turns the drum of the sexton and swings down to the horizon. He scribbles down: latitude 29 16.7 N, longitude: 0.38 05.7 E, and speed: 11.5 knots. The star gives him 52: 02.9. His face is bright in the torchlight. "I am only thirty miles out," he says. "Not bad in a little sea."

There are seven stars we can look at for their particular brightness and height, Double, Regulus, Alphard, Sirius, Rigel, Aldebaran and Capella. Ashley has spotted Scorpio and Orion's Belt. The skill is to triangulate the stars to have a feel for your position.

The stars, the sun and the moon would have been familiar to the Queen of Sheba. So would the perils that might obscure them. It is humid on the Red Sea and the evaporation can give false readings. What every sailor wants is a clear horizon. Tonight is a perfect night for the Queen of Sheba.

The sun rises on Egypt—we are about eighty miles east of the coast. The sun's oasis of light is on the starboard side, Saudi. The sea is empty of vessels and wildlife. No birds and too rough for fishing vessels. The crew has seen mostly Russian ships during the night—both merchant and military.

The story of the Queen of Sheba is the story of a journey. How you behave on the journey is character-forming.

It is starting to feel like home. The sailors are preparing for their Beirut stop. There is a routine: barber, postcards—never sent, and pub. In Bahrain, they got American jarhead cuts and are hoping for something slightly less severe in

Beirut. For women, hair is tied in a bun and must be of normal if not a natural colour. Makeup has to be minimal. No Queen of Sheba kohl eyes and heavy oils.

We are 200 miles from Suez. The end of the journey is in sight. Three more sunsets. This evening the sun fell early behind a cloud, so no J M W Turner sky, although the effect instead spread to the sea, which turned pinkish amid the ink blue. Starboard, sailors were gathering for a beer, a transition to home life.

At around 5:00 a.m. on Sunday, the ship parts company with the Queen of Sheba. She would have sailed off up the Gulf of Aqaba. We're going west, towards Suez. The rising sun lights the starboard sea behind us. Dragon sails north to the tip of the Red Sea. There is land—the Egyptian Shaker islands and Sinai. There are birds.

For a moment, I think I have spotted trees and picked up the binoculars. They are oil rigs. This is tanker country. We are forming of a convoy of ships towards Suez—at 8:00 p.m. we will anchor and await our slot. As the land looms closer—there are about thirteen nautical miles between Egypt and Sinai here—the threat of terrorism increases. The ship is reverting to a state of readiness to enter the canal.

Egypt portside has Old Testament shafts of light through cloud illuminating its coast. I think of Exodus 8, God to Moses: "And the Egyptians shall know that I am the Lord when I stretch forth mine hand upon Egypt and bring out the children of Israel from among them."

My adventure continues in Egypt. The crew of HMS Dragon are heading home for Portsmouth. But my sea quest is for knowledge. I want to test the claims that I have heard, that the clues to the Queen of Sheba lie in Egypt. More specifically, in the Temple of Hatshepsut in Luxor, once called Thebes.

Chapter 12

Egypt, February/March The Riddle of the Sphinx. Was the Queen of Sheba an Egyptian Pharoah?

My enthusiasm for travelling to Egypt can be traced to a conversation that I had at a British Museum dinner for trustees and friends earlier in the year.

The formal dinner was laid out in one of the museum's exhibition halls, and I was sitting next to Sir Paul Ruddock, a trustee of the British Museum, the V&A and the New York Met, who has donated millions to these and other charities. But our conversation was of a more personal nature. I brought up—of course—the Queen of Sheba and he cocked his head intently. By happy coincidence, he had a particular interest in both Israel and Ethiopia.

He listened closely as I told him my increasing vexations over getting dates to tally. Do Solomon and the Queen of Sheba definitely co-exist in the ninth–tenth centuries BC, and if so why is it so hard to find the evidence? The Egyptians have far more archival evidence for their lives, partly because of their obsession with the tombs.

Then Sir Paul tells me something that slightly makes the statues in the room spin. He knows a historian of ancient civilisations who believes that Solomon and the Queen of Sheba's dates are out of synch. His acquaintance reckons he has evidence that they actually existed 200 or 300 years later. As I leave the dinner, getting lost in halls of books and display cases of ancient marvels, I am determined to follow this new trail, even if it proves to be a path leading nowhere. The Queen of Sheba is more a mosaic than a route and I am discovering that every fragment of evidence is worth examining.

Two days later, I am in Maida Vale, not far from the Lord's cricket ground, in north-west London, looking for a mansion flat belonging to Michael Goldelman. The art dealer, historian and—in his worlds—'eternal scholar', turns out to be a puppyish figure. He has dark, precisely combed hair and thick glasses. On his table are two jars, one full of small boiled sweets, the other nearly empty of jelly babies. I go for the jelly babies and his rueful gaze follows me.

He shows me some striking artefacts, which he pulls out of boxes and unwraps from the kitchen roll. These include tiny faces that look almost Aztec like they are so brightly painted and exaggerated in expression. They are Phoenicians, from the land now mostly absorbed by Lebanon and Israel. They were the great traders and it was Hiram, the Phoenician king of Tyre, who sent the cedars and helped Solomon build his temple. His dates are given as approximately the middle of the tenth century, but—like so much else—there is no direct evidence for them.

According to Goldelman, we are too reliant on the Roman Jewish historian Titus Flavius Josephus, the first century AD recorder of Jewish history, The Jewish Antiquities. "He had a couple of Egyptian sources, but not Arabic sources. We know now more than he knew, he didn't have access to the Egyptian and Assyrian inscriptions," says Goldelman, just short of disdain.

He also had an interest in making the Jewish people as ancient as possible, so may have dated them generously. Even at his own age, Flavius was challenged. A rabbinical chronicle of the second century, Seder Olam Rabbah, dated the destruction of the first temple of Jerusalem as 352 BC rather than 586.

Now for Goldelman's own work: "I am doing a brand new theory; it is a new fashion, trying to re-adjust the chronology of the Near East."

Others have blazed this trail, including the Russian born psychiatrist Immanuel Velikovsky in his book *Ages in Chaos* (1952) and, later, Emmet Sweeney, the Scottish historian whose radical chronology theories include King Arthur and Atlantis. Velikovsky goes in for extreme re-dating with remarkable consequences. He suggests, for instance, that the Egyptian Eighteenth Dynasty, currently classified as the first dynasty of the New Kingdom of Egypt, when Egypt rose to its greatest power from 1550 to 1292 BC, actually existed at the same time as Solomon. This means that the great Queen of the Eighteenth Dynasty, Queen Hatshepsut, would have been a contemporary of King Solomon. And if that was the case, was she in fact the Queen of Sheba?

I've been looking for the elusive Queen of Sheba. Has she been sitting in plain sight all these years as another great historical figure? The Yemenis claim her. The Ethiopians claim her. Was she also an Egyptian?

Ethiopian and Arabian tradition is woven into the story of the Queen of Sheba. But I have learned already about the rich Egyptian influence. It is there in *Song of Songs*, the style of which can be traced to Egyptian love poems.

The most famous thing the world knows about Queen Hatshepsut—conventionally recorded as a pharaoh of the fifteenth century BC—is that she launched an expedition to a distant country known as Punt, or the Land of the God. Scholars have considered many locations for Punt, including Sudan and Somalia. Many have settled on Ethiopia—in those days it included the seacoast that is now Eritrea. In order for Hatshepsut's authority to be accepted in a patriarchal society, it is said she donned a beard. Just as the Queen of Sheba's hairy legs were a challenge to male authority.

My quest reaches the British ambassador who invites me, out of curiosity, to his residence in Cairo. Here are manicured lawns, faded ballrooms, photographs of the British Prime Minister Anthony Eden with his nemesis General Nasser, who humiliated the British and the French in the battle for Suez. We sip a glass of wine on the terrace of the fine white building and I tell him about my year-long journey in search of a 3,000-year-old queen. I tell him that, strange as it sounds, she is personal to me. I feel she has been a companion as well as a subject. She has made me more adventurous and more curious. Hard questions lead to a deeper thirst for knowledge.

He in turn says that I am right to look for female rulers in Egypt. Women have held great and mysterious power here. Also, he says that the Egyptians treasure both Queens and water. Back to the Dean of Canterbury Cathedral and his clue that the significance of the Queen of Sheba lies in the sea.

The Nile is the lifeblood of the country, a patchwork of green running alongside in a land of desert. The ambassador explains the tension between Egypt and Ethiopia over the building of a dam in the Ethiopian stretch of the Blue Nile. Will it take water levels from the Egyptian side? I tell him about the Utopia of fertile land which was Saba and how it was thought to be in Yemen because of the Marib dam. The politics of water is ancient and modern.

Before travelling to Upper Egypt in search of the great Pharaoh Hatshepsut perhaps close to our Queen of Sheba, I go north to Alexandria, home to Cleopatra who lived in the first century BC, nearly a millennium later than the Queen of Sheba and 1,500 years later than Hatshepsut.

Archaeologists are planning to excavate Alexandria's lovely harbour onto the Mediterranean. Their dream is to find there Cleopatra's temple. Another trading port, Another queen. Another visceral link to the Queen of Sheba.

This is the description in Shakespeare's Antony and Cleopatra, of the first sighting of the Egyptian queen. In Act 11, scene 11, Enobarbus says:

"I will tell you, the barge she sat in, like a burnish'd throne,
Burned on the water: the poop was beaten gold;
Purple the sails, and so perfumed that
The winds were lovesick with them; the oars
Were silver,
Which to the tune of flutes kept stroke, and made
The water which they beat to follow faster,
As amorous of their strokes. For her own person,
It beggar'd all description: she did lie
In her pavilion, cloth of gold of tissue..."

An exotically beautiful queen arrives in naval splendour to embark on a dazzling love affair. The resonance need not be spelt out. Cleopatra had something else in common with the Queen of Sheba. She has a legacy as a dangerous temptress, although historically she had a more serious role as the last ruler of the Ptolemaic kingdom of Egypt.

Hatshepsut fits into the picture as a kind of role model for both queens. She ruled against the odds, by claiming that her father was Amun, a god.

Just to make sure, she carved proclamations from Amun on her monuments:

"Welcome my sweet daughter, my favourite, the King of Upper and Lower Egypt, Hatshepsut. Thou are the Pharaoh, taking possession of Two Lands."

She also juggled dynasty by co-ruling with her nephew Thutmose 111 for about twenty years. Her miscalculation was to try to rid herself of him by sending him off to war. He returned victoriously and his revenge was spectacular, smashing up her monuments and chiselling out her images.

But apart from her wicked aunt status, she was a great ruler. Her first love was trade and her extraordinary achievement was to launch the expedition of Punt, to the Horn of Africa. She wanted frankincense trees, animals, treasure, knowledge. She was, in her fashion, a forerunner to Napoleon. She is certainly a forerunner if not something closer to the Queen of Sheba.

I take a flight to Luxor, the Valley of the Kings and the site of Queen Hatshepsut's famous Temple. I have come to see the fresco of the Expedition of Punt, much damaged by her enraged nephew but remarkable nevertheless.

Her purpose was to eclipse the male pharaohs. Their tombs were hidden in the sand. Her temple is elegantly and symmetrically carved into the mountain rock, so you cannot see from the distant shape where the temple ends and the hill begins.

I book into the Winter Palace, in Luxor, formerly Thebes, a town that would have been known to the Queen of Sheba. The hotel is famous for its sweeping staircase, for it was here that Howard Carter announced his discovery of treasures of Tutankhamen, in November 1922.

There are large tended gardens outside, watered, the grass soft underfoot. I can imagine the Queen of Sheba trailed by birds and animals, in an oasis of her own making. My phone buzzes—it is serendipitously an email from my husband with pictures of reeds and lily pads. He has started to dig a pond for me in our garden in Norfolk. I smile and feel my first wave of homesickness. This journey has led me away from my life but I see now how it might make me appreciate more.

As the afternoon sun blazes over the Nile, I take a boat across the Nile to the West Bank. East bank for the living, west bank for the dead. The boatman does not much look like Charon, the ferryman from Hades in Greek mythology who carries across the souls of the dead. My ferry has a mat saying welcome and is decorated with flags. My guide is a gentle, barely audible Egyptologist who is happy to look at tombs for the rest of his life. He says that we must acknowledge death in order to understand the meaning of life.

I tell him about the singular purpose of my visit: the Temple of Hatshepsut. Some things should be savoured—I want to just stand and stare. The dimensions, the colours of the limestone temple against the limestone and sandstone mountain rocks. Hatshepsut chose this spot with her architect, Senenmut and forbade any nearby tombs.

The only person permitted to be buried here was the architect himself. Luxor gossip is that Hatshepsut was so pleased with the building that she became a lover of her architect. Hatshepsut knew that the sun would rise in the east before her and set in the west behind the mountain. The harmony of symmetry is also a matter of religious faith. The ancient Egyptians believed that the journey through the underworld took place at night, a dangerous journey passing crocodiles and demons. Only the *Book of the Dead* could protect you. Dawn was the time of re-birth.

I arrive mid-afternoon and can see the light and shadows in play over the mountain. As Hatshepsut looked back she would have seen the green lands of the Nile Delta spreading uninterrupted before her.

The Temple is in three layers and composed of perfect columns. It exists in splendid isolation. Above it only the mountain, the skies, and screeching swifts circling.

At the base on the right hand is a sphinx, with the bearded head of Hatshepsut. The top half of the head is smashed, as are many of the sculptures of her here, but you can see one gazing eye and a half-smile on full lips.

On the other side of the base to the ramp-up to the upper floors, is the root of a frankincense tree. This was the prized spoil from the exhibition of Punt. Hatshepsut needed frankincense in her own country and was determined to grow it in Thebes. A sign says: "This tree was brought from Punt by Hatshepsut's expedition."

The early season clumps of tourists are heading up the ramp. My guide indicated that I should stay.

"Here, you can see what you came for, all by yourself." I walk dreamily towards the first row of columns and there in front of me is the story of the Punt expedition. The longer you stare, the more the shapes become apparent. It is an exuberant adventure.

The sea is drawn in zigzag lines and sea creatures pass through it. My guide says almost thirteen in all, including a catfish and a lobster. There is a turtle swimming beneath a carved palm tree, a curved roofed dwelling and a ladder. There are more trees that look as if they are frankincense. There is a carving of a donkey setting out on board. I am reminded of the debate of whether the Queen of Sheba travelled by domestic camel, or if she would have, according to dates, have gone by donkey. Next to it, is a woman of swollen belly, recorded in the guide books as African. Was she carried somewhere by the donkey?

I peer closer at the stone. There are flashes of colour, mostly a rust-red that has somehow survived desecration. There are some pots and rings and, if look very carefully the shape of giraffe towers of them. There is an outline of a leopard. The ship must have looked a little like Noah's Ark as it returned from Punt.

A row of aquamarine zigzags higher up the wall, looks like the return journey, as Egyptian figures load up the gangplank. In another scene, the rowers are at full stroke, braced for the Red Sea currents that HMS Dragon can surge through. The colour returns for the great mounds of henna on board, alongside more depictions of frankincense trees—this time in pots, to keep the roots moist. The Queen of Sheba loved henna as did Hatshepsut.

One of the Queen of Sheba's riddles to Solomon was about henna. At the end of the line, lions walk proudly beneath a throne, and a line of mustard yellow and red ends the fresco. The figure on the throne—Hatshepsut—has been chiselled out assiduously. The lobster and the catfish survived her nephew, but not his loathed aunt.

I have lingered so long in front of the Punt expedition frieze that the sun is starting to drop at the side of the mountain. I hurriedly climb the ramp and look down at the soft late afternoon light on the land towards the Nile and the East Bank beyond, from my elevated terrace.

Above me are the several remaining great statues of Hatshepsut. Her arms are crossed over her unseen breasts, her artificial beard like an enlarged tongue or phallus from chin to chest. Her Pharaoh's hat looks like wizardry. She is as imposing and as lasting as the mountain. Her sightless eyes look like prophecy. I reach the highest level and crane my neck towards the top of the mountain rock and the swooping swifts in the dusk sky.

It is becoming cool and the guide tells me that I cannot stay any longer, the temple is about to close. The boatman is waiting. So I cross the Nile by sunset thinking more about my warship. Both Hatshepsut and the Queen of Sheba believed that a great journey on the Red Sea was destiny for them. Both mastered power, trade and foreign policy.

Was there more to it than that?

Hatshepsut is known for two things: first, her great sea voyage to Punt, with a fleet of five seventy-feet ships with sails; her ships return laden with treasure, myrrh, frankincense and henna/ kohl eyeliner.

Second is the construction of palaces. Hatshepsut's sublime temple, whose ancient name was 'the most sacred of sacred places', is a temple of perfect symmetry, with terraces leading to an inner sanctum. Could this have been modelled on Solomon's Temple? Could Solomon's Temple have been modelled on Hatshepsut's Temple?

Emmet Sweeney claims she was of mixed race. She also claimed part divinity—a union between her mother and Amun, just as the Queen of Sheba was reputed to have an element of jinn.

Sweeney triumphantly claims over our Skype conversation that Hatshepsut resembles the Queen of Sheba once the jigsaw is in place. He further claims— and it is a singular view—that Punt is not in face Ethiopia and Eritrea, but the

Jordan Valley, by the Dead Sea. The valley now forms the border between Jordan and Israel and the West Bank.

He has an answer for critics who point out that on the picture reliefs of the Punt expedition there are wild animals—giraffes, lions—and that frankincense comes from Yemen and Ethiopia. He says that the Sahara and Arabia would have been more of savannah in the first century BC, and that rock drawings show people hunting giraffes. Indeed, he says the desertification of the Sahara and Arabia began in the third millennium BC. He says many of the African creatures depicted on Hatshepsut's temple still roamed around the tropical Jordan Valley/Dead Sea in Hatshepsut's time.

He sends a further, lengthy email with pointers 'completely ignored in mainstream publications'. What of the evidence that Puntites on the shore region (widely thought to be the Eritrean coast) lived in houses on stilts—which points to Africa? Sweeney has found stilt houses on Hatshepsut's monuments which evoke the northern shore of the Gulf of Aqaba.

He writes: "Eilat sits in what might be described as a funnel and is even today subject to flash flooding from wadis originating in the Sinai mountains to the west and the Edom mountains to the east, as well as the Negev uplands from the north." The water is directed into the Eilat area. "In antiquity, it would have been extremely sensible for the inhabitants of the region to construct their homes on stilts."

Sweeney says that the Punt expedition must have been a pilgrimage. But later the language describing it became more tender and personal. "It was a lover's language," he says. "I do believe that she and the King of Jerusalem had an affair." He claims that the phrases in *Song of Songs* are identical to those which appear on Hatshepsut's monument, the Mortuary Temple at Deir el-Bahari near the Valley of the Kings.

Hatshepsut writes that her limbs were 'fragrant with the incense of Punt'. In *Song of Songs*, the lover's limbs are 'fragrant with incense'. A Punt is described as 'a place of delight' echoing the ecstasy of *Song of Songs*. And there is the reference to the Pharaoh's horses in *Song of Songs*. "I have compared thee, O my love, to a company of horses in Pharaoh's chariots."

Then there is the name Makeda, used by the Ethiopians for the Queen of Sheba. "It is strikingly similar to Hatshepsut's throne name of Makera ('Truth of the spirit of Ra')."

But why the confusion over D and R? The ancient Phoenician alphabet, also used in Israel, had a similar triangular symbol for the two letters. "*The Kebra*

Nagast derived from many sources, including Israel and Egypt, so presumably some scribe could have read the Queen of Sheba's name Makera and Makeda."

As I close my computer, I suddenly remember Josephus the Roman historian's reference to the Queen of Egypt and Ethiopia. The women are also bound by the serpent worship of their cultures. The Queen of Sheba was said to be descended from serpent kings. Serpents are linked to divinity in Egypt.

The Queen of Sheba has the characteristics of a priestess as well as a Queen. She is unfolding before me. I think again of the serpents. I have come across them, with the frankincense trees of Oman. It is a local legend that the trees were protected by flying snakes. The flying snakes are an interesting example of eastern and rabbinic folklore merging. They are also, as with so much in the Queen of Sheba legend, ambiguous. Are they good or bad?

There is one final link between Hatshepsut and the Queen of Sheba. Solomon is said to have had one daughter of a Pharaoh as a wife—she features in Arab tradition as a temptress who persuades him to worship false gods, leading to his falling out of favour with the Old Testament God and therefore losing his power and kingdom. Could he have had two, or is Hatshepsut a conflation of Solomon's pharaoh wife and of the Queen of Sheba?

But if Sweeney is so sure that his theory fits, why can't he convince others of it? He claims it is the unwillingness of the Egyptologists to throw out their canon of work. "It means whole textbooks, whole segments of libraries are wrong. The most closed mind people I have met in any discipline are the Egyptologists. They won't even listen to the argument. I have a mountain to climb. They will find one detail and all the other evidence becomes ignored."

I hear from Sweeney again, out of the blue, in 2020. He has a theory about the pandemic.

Hi Sarah,

Just saw a post on Facebook which noted that Ireland's Covid-19 death rate has doubled since they started vaccinating. Pretty sure it's the same everywhere. This is fast developing into a major crime against humanity. Wonder if anyone will ever be held accountable.

Aha. It's a hoax.

"Yes, Sarah, the Covid-19 hoax is utterly sinister. We can only pray common sense will prevail before the country—and the entire Western world—is ruined beyond repair."

The 'conspiracy' of Covid-19 turns out to be related to the archaeological conspiracy against Hatshepsut.

Like the 'science' between Covid-19, Egyptian chronology has no scientific basis whatsoever and is ultimately based on the chronology of the bible and the assumed date of Adam and Eve.

The Queen of Sheba is a legend, muse and conspiracy. Have we invented her to meet our myriad needs? To me, she is still the tiny figure in Claude Lorrain's The Embarkation of the Queen of Sheba. She is a journey, and I must complete mine.

Chapter 13
Gulf of Aqaba, March Sailing into the Port of Solomon, the End of the Sea Journey

I meet the Queen of Sheba again at the Gulf of Aqaba for the final stage of her journey to Jerusalem. I have her sailing into Solomon's port—from which he sent out ships to fetch the gold, silver, sandalwood, pearls, ivory, apes, and peacocks of the mysterious African port of Ophir—as if Ophir itself were arriving.

Most archaeologists place the ancient port here, though it is hard immediately to imagine it, under the tall hotels and holiday resort sprawl of Eilat. From what was once called Ezion-Geber I reckon she can lead a procession of camels to Jerusalem up the Negev Valley.

The Gulf of Aqaba is the beginning of the glory of Solomon. There is copper ore in the Wadi Arabah and somewhere around here—exactly where is a matter of exciting new research—was the centre of the copper industry, the origins of Solomon's fabulous wealth, literally King Solomon's mines. I have been cautious about historical sources for the Queen of Sheba but the archaeological breakthrough on the Negev mines equals the excitement of the ancient temple of Yeha in Northern Ethiopia.

According to the Bible, copper funded "a navy of ships in Ezion-Geber which is beside Eloth, on the shore of the Red Sea, in the land of Edom." From here ships voyaged to the fabled Ophir—a place still to be identified by archaeologists—and "fetched from thence gold, 420 talents and brought it to King Solomon."

We know how copper impressed observers. Here is the Bible on the impact of the work of Hiram of Tyre, Phoenicia (now Lebanon) who supervised the construction of Solomon's temple and was a master coppersmith. "All the vessels which Hiram made for King Solomon in the temple of the Lord were of burnished copper. In the plain of Jordan did the kin have them cast" (1 Kings 7: 45–46).

Excavations nearby by the late archaeologist Nelson Glueck included fragments of a large storage jar, inscribed with southern Arabic letters. He speculated that it could have been a container of precious products brought from southern Arabia. In addition to huge jars filled with the extremely valuable spices and incense, she apparently brought with her 'very much gold and precious stones'. Glueck concluded: "Among the goods that Solomon must have given her in exchange, there were probably some of the copper and iron products of the Arabah and Ezion-Geber."

Here is the evidence of the trade between the Queen of Sheba and King Solomon. She came as a hard-headed businesswoman as well as a foreign queen.

I fly in from Tel Aviv and walk down to the front. From the jetty by the seaside cafes, you can understand the true sweep of the gulf, Jordan on the east side, Eilat to the west. As I look across from Eilat I see the great flag of the Arab revolt against the Ottoman empire, commemorating the Battle of Aqaba in 1917, in which the British soldier, archaeologist and adventurer T E Lawrence—Lawrence of Arabia—took part.

The flag flies 130 metres high, dominating the harbour. Behind it is a white mosque. Distantly, I can hear the call to prayer, in contrast to the disco music of the Eilat bars. As the sun sets over the mountains of Eilat, it lights up the Edomite Mountains of Jordan in pink, graceful blush. An oil tanker crosses the coast in the distance, beyond the embers of the sun's path. It is a splendid gulf, at which two civilisations meet—Judaic and Islamic. The Negev Valley is the same land.

I'm in the Queen of Sheba hotel, a close neighbour of the Solomon hotel. It is a giant tourist hotel, but there are stone friezes in the lobby and the bathroom toiletries are a Sheba range, which I reckon she would have appreciated. We know from the poetry that the Queen of Sheba smelt good.

I order a Queen of Sheba salad, which is more or less a Caesar, and eat Queen of Sheba caramel chocolates, extra-large chocolate drops. Through the windows comes the thud of a disco beat. Miami style lights flash through the curtains. The curving silhouettes of the mountains around the port speak of another time. Across the sea, I can make out the lights of a ship.

The border crossing between Israel and Jordan is open from 7:30 a.m. to 7:30 p.m., allowing the Jordanians who work in the Eilat hotels to come and go on day returns, walking more urgently than the travellers with rucksacks who amble talkatively across the no man's land between the high barbed-wire fences. The

154

Israelis are searching in their security questions—I find even repeating my name becomes a test of behavioural psychology. Both sides benefit handsomely from cash visas. There are photographs at security checks of President Clinton, Prime Minister Rabin of Israel and King Hussein of Jordan signing the peace treaty here in 1994.

My Jordanian driver Mohamed is a computer science graduate who cannot find work in his field. He plays Jordanian music on his car radio, but the station tends to shift to an Israeli wavelength, owing to the close proximity of Jordan's neighbour. Unemployment is high and I see scores of young men sitting around the centre of Aqabah.

We drive down to the port and look back at Eilat, just as I looked over to Jordan the evening before. A Jordanian naval vessel patrols an invisible line in the stirringly lovely horseshoe gulf. From here, you can see Israel and Egypt. Suez is about an hour by boat. The Saudi border is only six miles from here along the sandy road.

Mohamed plans his Hajj—pilgrimage—to Mecca next Ramadan. Those who remain doubtful about the view that the Queen of Sheba travelled by sea would like to think of the Queen of Sheba making the arduous journey in reverse—coming up by caravan from southern Arabia across the Empty Quarter. Here, at this point, I can see the breadth of her journey and its end.

We walk out along a jetty, from which the lands of Egypt and Israel are in a sun haze of limestone and dark sandstone mountains. The Red Sea swells across the four lands. I ask Mohamad about the seasonal winds that could have blown the Queen of Sheba away from the shore. He says the winds are never so powerful here. It is sand and sky. A father is swimming with his son at the jetty, the boy diving in and out of the clear water like a heron.

I hope here to find evidence of Tell el Kheleifeh, the site excavated by the twentieth-century archaeologist Nelson Glueck, who uncovered not only copper but a Solomonic fortress and harbour for his ships—the fabled Ezion Geber. But the site appears to be a development for a five-star lagoon complex called Ayla. Luxury has different meanings in different ages.

The trouble with the history of Solomon and the Queen of Sheba is that history can be elusive. Glueck believed his excavation was of the tenth century BC. Other archaeologists cast doubt on this. As one of Glueck's colleagues later said: "We did the best we could with the methods then available to us."

Solomon and his successors maintained fortresses and industrial settlements even in the almost completely arid Southern Negev, to protect the trade routes through it between Jerusalem and the port of Ezion-Geber (Eilat).

Glueck believed that the Negev provided the evidence for King Solomon's might and prosperity—and a kingdom that ran in a peaceful, law-abiding manner. The Bible described it like this: "And Judah and Israel dwelt safely, every man under his vine and fig tree, from Dan even unto Beersheba, all the days of Solomon" (1 Kings 4:25).

So we can imagine the Negev south of Beersheba that was strategically important, with highways to Egypt and to the Red Sea and a Wadi Arabah rich in copper.

Those mines are looking increasingly real. There is increasing historical evidence of them. The Arabic name of the copper mine site in the Wadi Arabah is Khirbet Nahas (The Copper Ruin) likely to be the Ir Nahash (The City of Copper) mentioned in the Bible. The Promised Land of Deuteronomy 8:9 describes a land "whose stones are iron and out of whose hills thou canst dig copper."

The history of archaeology is as layered as geology. Glueck was accompanied in his work by a photographer called Beno Rothenberg, a mathematician and philosopher by training. He was there when Glueck pronounced Timna Valley in southern Israel—about eighteen miles north of Aqaba—Solomonic. Rothenberg became a champion of archaeometallurgy, the significance of metal in getting evidence of ancient history.

It is metallurgy that led to a breakthrough at Timna in establishing the clues of the Iron Age—eleventh to ninth centuries BC, and therefore the evidence for Solomon's Mines in the biblically correct period. Rothenberg died in 2012, but his work was taken up by another professor.

He is called Erez Ben-Yosef and he works at the archaeology department of Tel Aviv University. He is a muscular, dark-haired, cheerful man striding about in shorts. He is in high spirits, for he had been responsible for a rare and genuine breakthrough working in the field of metal and excavating in southern Israel.

Until recently, there was no significant archaeology from the tenth century BC, the period in which, according to the Bible, the area south of the Dead sea was conquered by David. 2 Samuel 8: 13–14. "And David became famous after he returned from striking down 18,000 Edomites in the valley of salt. He put garrisons throughout Edom and all the Edomites became subject to David."

Professor Ben-Yosef found remains of fortifications dated from exactly this period within the Timna valley, near to Eilat. In the slag mounds at a place called Slaves Hill, he found evidence of metal production that dated to the tenth century BC, surrounded by walls.

Has the Tel Aviv professor found King Solomon's mines?

Professor Erez Ben-Josef had been piecing together the archaeological evidence. The conditions were serendipitous. The desert is dry, and thus archaeological evidence is remarkably preserved. Here was proof of textile dyeing from plants, and a rich diet seen through animal fossils. Grape, fig, pomegranate, almonds, pistachio, olives. Furthermore, he had found the remains of a pregnant woman entombed nearby. This suggested, did it not, that women had a role during these times, they were part of the arduous expeditions to the copper mines.

As for the fruits, these were not local produce but had been brought on a trade route. This was Arabian trade, brought by a caravan. I can almost feel the dust of the great caravan of the Queen of Sheba.

The Timna site in the Israeli Negev has yielded not only evidence of civilisation but also, heart-skippingly for my purposes, of a camel trail. It was in the tenth century that the first domesticated camels started to appear: perhaps the Queen of Sheba was a pioneer.

This is wonderful news. The Queen of Sheba could have unloaded at Eilat and completed her journey to Jerusalem by camel caravan. She is becoming real again.

Now I am back in Israel I go to Timna Park and meet the grizzled desert guide, Assaf Holzer. The park is a natural marvel—a valley in a range of granite, limestone, sandstone, where copper has been mined in the ancient world. The copper here differs from that on the Jordan side of the border, being closer to the surface because of erosion and exposure. Assaf leads me to look at some vertical mine shafts, with evidence of hacking marks from chisels.

The influences here are Egyptian—famously a rock drawing of Ramses III—but Professor Erez Ben Josef has also been able to use carbon dating to prove Glueck's theory in the 1950s that this was the tenth century, and thus has a claim to be Solomon's mines. Indeed this discovery is more exciting than the work Glueck was doing in the Jordanian Edomite Mountains. The dates there are harder to prove.

Then Assaf takes me to Slaves' Hill, which is Professor Erez's own patch. There are walls here, but no fortresses. That suggests a period of peaceful prosperity, trade rather than conflict. As for the name 'Slaves Hill', Erez has doubts. There is evidence of finer food, bones of goats and sheep. There is a clearing for donkeys and even evidence of donkey feed. Erez believes these were the quarters of the skilled masons and engineers, mining experts.

This was the centre of the copper industry. You can still see the slag forced out by the furnaces and remains of charcoal scattered across the bottom of the hill. We drive along the stony valley road to look at the so-called Solomon pillars—magnificent boulders of layered stone, which are naturally made and certainly pre-date Solomon. So does what looks almost like the head of a sphinx, carved by geology.

Assaf says he has heard tour guides insouciantly ascribing Solomon's pillars to the king, but in fact, there is something historic here and much more exciting. There was a copper mining industry here in the tenth century? Why? Who ran it? This is where you get into the politics of biblical archaeology.

That these were under the control of Solomon would explain his fabled wealth and the importance of a trade route through this valley. There is no local source of water, although there was a spring about eight miles north which could have been the watering stop. But there have been found the remains of fish bones here from the ancient world—fish not from the Red Sea or the Nile, but from the Mediterranean. The juniper and oak found here are believed to have come from Jordan. The Egyptians would have needed copper for the pivots of their chariots. Surely this was a trade route.

Glueck pictured a bustling, cosmopolitan highway: "Merchants and royal messengers, soldiers and missionaries and pilgrims, itinerant smiths, artists and musicians passed busily to and from with their goods or instruments along the travel routes that bound the Byzantine world together.

"The exotic products of Arabia Felix, Ethiopia and other Eastern lands were in especially high demand and in the very considerable measure were transported across the convenient crossroads of the Negev." There was surely room for a queen.

Many years later, the Negev was to become an exuberant hub of the Byzantine economy. During the fifth and sixth centuries AD, silks, silver, ivory, gold, incense, perfumes, ebony, cosmetics and salt came this way, exchanged for the more practical commodities of tools, metal, weapons, cloth, oil, wine and wheat.

The Negev is important for Jews, Christians and Muslims. This was the land into which Abraham and his people travelled and where Abraham offered his

son Isaac as a sacrifice to God and was shown mercy. "Abraham turned back...
and they arose and went together to Beersheba where Abraham took up his
abode" (Genesis 22:19).

Hagar, Abraham's mistress and maid to his wife Sarah, sought refuge here
and gave birth to his child Ishmael, from whom Islam is derived. Solomon's
father David, shepherd son of Jesse, sought refuge in the Negev when his patron
Saul turned against him. He was offered sanctuary north of Beersheba by the
Philistine king Achish.

I leave the dramatic shapes and colours of the Negev—once volcanic, once
oceanic—and head back to Eilat. This has been a satisfying trip. For the first
time, I have seen historical evidence for the existence of Solomon. These were
not the fabled Solomon's Mines of popular stories. Somewhere in Africa perhaps
mines of gold and diamonds are still to be discovered, just as we shall one day
establish the location of Ophir. But they are real mines that fit the period
associated with the king of Israel. The closer we get to Solomon, the more we
reach the Queen of Sheba.

It's possible that she travelled by a different route—an Egyptian trade route
ran through the Sinai—but I like to think of her going through the Negev, a great
queen travelling in safety thanks to the security imposed on an important
industrial area by a mighty king.

It is time for the final part of my journey. It is the moment for the Queen of
Sheba to enter Jerusalem. I have experienced her as a metaphor for trade, love,
or the church. Now she feels visible flesh. A great Queen heading towards her
destiny.

Am I going to be any the wiser, in Jerusalem?

Chapter 14

Jerusalem, March The Entrance of the Queen of Sheba. Journey's End

At last, Jerusalem. The shining city on the hill, translucent, iridescent, faith embedded in its foundations, every stone a story. The grassy mounds and lines of cypress and olive trees beyond the walls only thrown into sharper relief the paleness of Jerusalem.

Even the afternoon sky is snow top white with just a band of gold for cloud cover.

It is a city of pilgrimage. The faithful expand, orthodox Jews hurrying towards the gates, Muslims overcome at the proximity of the Al Aqsa mosque. I feel that I am on my pilgrimage too. The flickering of faith, intermittently doused by scepticism, becomes a warm internal glow. I cannot take my eyes from the golden Dome, its orb lights the city as if the sun.

I can see why a pagan queen might have renounced her gods for this. I understand why the Mappa Mundi placed Jerusalem as the capital of the world. I know why the Queen of Sheba was said to take her place at the end of time here. Humankind will fight to the death for their plot of heaven on earth.

I remember Matthew, Gospels 12: "On Judgement Day the Queen of the South will rise up with this generation and condemn it because she came from the ends of the earth to hear the Wisdom of Solomon and there is something greater than Solomon here."

I look up the words of Rabbinic literature:

> "As the navel is set in the centre of the human body, so is the land of Israel the navel of the world...
> situated in the centre of the world,
> and Jerusalem in the centre of the land of Israel,

and the sanctuary in the centre of Jerusalem,
and the holy place in the centre of the sanctuary,
and the ark in the centre of the holy place,
and the foundation stone before the holy place,
because from it the world was founded."

The story of Jerusalem is woven into the legend of the Queen of Sheba.

As I wander through the Jewish, Muslim, Armenian quarters of the Old City what I see and smell is the spices; the bowls of spices and fruits. Myrrh, saffron, patchouli, amber, and little rocks of frankincense. I turn up the Via Dolorosa; the narrow street marking the final Stations of the Cross that Jesus is believed to have carried from Calvary to Golgotha. I walk through the little Coptic Church that leads to the Holy Sepulchre and into an atmosphere that is thick with the cloying scent. The Magi, including the Ethiopian king, brought gifts of gold, myrrh and frankincense to celebrate Christ's birth. Here I smell the last of those at this place of his execution.

A year ago, my quest for the Queen of Sheba began in Axum, Ethiopia, which considers itself a second Jerusalem. Here I am in Axum's inspiration. The city walls, built by the Ottomans on top of earlier fortifications, take on an eternal quality in the milky afternoon light. The old limestone city gleams. It is quiet except for the rising sound of Muslim prayer.

This is a city of layered history. A cross-section of a single part finds stones of ancient Israel buried beneath construction work of the Hellenistic period, the foundations of the Roman Herodian wall and adaptations through the Byzantine, Islamic, Ayyubid and Ottoman periods.

When I walk down the remains of the Cardo—the commercial Roman road that once ran through the city, with pillared shops on either side—I find a glass-topped excavation that promises sections of the city wall of the period of the First Temple, below. I press my face to the glass but, peering into the darkness, I am not sure what I am looking at.

Naturally, I want to see the site supposed once to have housed Solomon's Temple, for there, surely, walked the Queen of Sheba. But Temple Mount is now a profoundly significant Islamic site and access is open to non-Muslims only in the early morning.

I return at 7:30 a.m., along empty cobbled limestone passages, to the security check at the Bab al-Magharibeh entrance.

Devout Jews are already at prayer at the Western Wall, the closest they can get to pray at this historical site. They bow in front of the great blocks of masonry, precisely laid to the specifications of Roman engineers as foundations for an enlarged mount area in the time of Herod.

And on to the Temple Mount itself, as the rising sun warms the stone courtyard. There is a moment of embarrassment as one of the mosque attendants' gestures at me: my skirt is modest but I have bare ankles. He sends me back to the entrance, where another attendant hands me a full length, elasticated black skirt.

My female Muslim guide stands with me before the grey dome of the Al Aqsa mosque, the third most holy site for Muslims after Mecca and Medina. To the left is the burnished gold of the Dome of the Rock, shining particularly brightly beneath the cobalt early morning sky.

This is the site at which Abraham was said to have been ready to sacrifice his son Isaac. It is also where Mohammed is said to have begun his journey to heaven. It is the centre of the world for Jews.

I am looking at the nearest point to heaven on earth. At the final day of reckoning, it is said that a chain from the Mount of Olives to the Dome of the Rock will appear. Those of the Muslim faith will reach the Dome, the rest will fall.

The creator of the Dome of the Rock was Abd al-Malik, commander of Jerusalem and Damascus from 685. A golden dome on octagonal walls. The Rock marked Adam's paradise, Abraham's altar and the site where David and Solomon planned their temple later, seen by Muhammad on his Night Journey.

For Muslims, Jerusalem was saved from the Crusaders by Saladin.

Saladin inspired history, just as Solomon—Suleiman—stretched across faith mythology. In the Middle Ages in Europe, Solomon became an inspiration for leaders such as Charlemagne. But the potency of the legend stretched to Arabia and North Africa and became part of Islamic tradition. Suleiman is regarded as one of the four great men of history; Suleiman, Nimrud (son of Cush, great-grandson of Noah) Nebuchadnezzar and Alexander the Great.

The prize of Jerusalem is intimately connected to Ark of the Covenant in the story of Solomon and Sheba. It gives divine favour and legitimacy. Solomon's Temple is built to house the Ark. It is sacred law, associated with the pure model of the monarchy. It is the revelation of God. If the Queen of Sheba can be regarded as an early pilgrim, millions were to follow from all religions.

When the British forces entered the city in November 1917 it was the first time that a Christian country had taken control of the city since the Crusades. In November 1917, Britain issued the Balfour Declaration, favouring the establishment of a Jewish state in Palestine but also committed to the religious rights of non-Jewish communities in Palestine. For Jews, this was an act of fairness; Muslims called it the catastrophe.

But when the Queen of Sheba arrived here 3,000 years ago, it was a place of peaceful splendour and religious unity. Solomon—Suleiman—claimed by both. I am melancholy that the Queen of Sheba came from a peaceful land to a reconciled city. Now Yemen is in an agony of civil war. Israel and Palestine are not at peace.

The faiths here are deep and volatile but they co-exist. As I leave the Temple Mount, past a group of Israeli soldiers guarding one of the several entrances from the old city that the Muslims can use, I smell newly baked bread. Shutters are opening and traders are putting out their bowls of spices and fruits. Commerce, trade, the exchange of goods. It made the world go around 3,000 years ago. It makes the world go round now.

I turn up the Via Dolorosa, putting out my hand to caress the markings of the Stations of the Cross, the episodes that marked Jesus's last day before his crucifixion, the sites that are now places of pilgrimage for the devout.

I enter the Holy Sepulchre and climb the steep staircase to the altar that symbolises the grief of Mary. Below, pilgrims gather at the Stone of the Anointment, a simple slab, said to be where Jesus's body was wrapped. Finally, I find myself in the small, silent shrine that contains the 14th Station of the Cross, the tomb of Jesus. I lay my hand on the worn smooth surface stone and bow my head. This is my pilgrimage.

We might see the Queen of Sheba as one of the first pilgrims, even before Mohammed and Christ. I leave the old city in the early evening along King David's route, up to the museums and the government quarter. The clouds are pastel blues and pinks and the Ottoman walls are backlit as I glance back.

I am heading towards the Bible Lands Museum. By coincidence, the curator Dr Yigal Bloch is planning an exhibition on the Queen of Sheba. It covers the period and the geography of the ancient Near East.

Here are artefacts, seals and inscriptions from Egypt, Assyria, Phoenicia, Babylonia, Persia, Israel and Judea. I see the pillar figurines—the women with curved arms cupping their breasts—from Syria, the model boat from the Egyptian Middle Kingdom, the shell-shaped boat from Sardinia, 800–700 BC, the stone block bearing the invocation of a curse by YHWH, from Judah, 800–700 BC. At the centre of the museum is a model of Jerusalem during the First Temple—Solomonic—period.

The case behind the model of Jerusalem depicts the monotheistic God of the Israelites but also some neighbouring deities. Here are the storm gods Baal and Haddad. And here are the goddesses. Ashrah, the mother goddess.

Was she the model for an allegorical Queen of Sheba? The war goddesses Anat and Astarte were established within the Levant and Egypt. There was Tanit, a bloodthirsty goddess, who demanded the sacrifice of children. In the ruins of Carthage (modern Tunisia), archaeologists found hundreds of urns containing the cremated bones of babies and children. Above the burial ground is a stele with an inscription dedicated to Tanit. Is she another version of the dreadful Lilith?

Dr Bloch, with greying hair and glasses, wears a preoccupied air. He takes me through the pristine glass and stone galleries to his cramped office, where the Queen of Sheba exhibition is being planned. It becomes clear that Dr Bloch, for all his learning and expressive eyebrows, cannot say whether or not the Queen of Sheba actually existed. I am beginning to worry that it is a law of erudition that those closest to the historical evidence remain the most sceptical. He believes that she is most likely a literary figure.

He thinks the biblical image of the Queen of Sheba was based on a North Arabian queen. She may be Samsi, who ruled lands to the west of Assyria and is mentioned in Assyrian royal inscriptions from the eighth century, specifically in the reigns of Tiglath-pileser 111 and Sargon 11.

There is no evidence of southern Arabian queens who match the Queen of Sheba's even most approximate dates. He is convinced that Solomon existed, although there is no more evidence for him outside the Bible than there is for the Queen of Sheba. He suggests that the land of Ophir—the source of those valuable cargoes that came to Jerusalem every few years—was likely to have been East Africa, Ethiopia.

I have learned by now that people see their own reflection of the Queen of Sheba. Perhaps this is the riddle of the glass floor. Not everything is as it appears. You see what you think you see. I have met clever historians, archaeologists and historians but I can find no consensus on the Queen of Sheba.

In this city of religions, I believe that she must be taken on faith. As the Ethiopian clergy say of the Ark of the Covenant: Believe it or don't believe it, we have it.

Dr Bloch and I are on the more genial ground when I ask him how he thinks the Queen of Sheba got to Jerusalem. Everybody has a view on directions and the best method of transport. Since Dr Bloch is speaking mainly to an audience of Yemeni Jews, he favours a desert overland trip.

Therefore it must be a camel route across the Arabian Peninsula, passing through Dedan, the territory to the north of the half of Saba that is in Arabia. I venture that the southern Arabians were settled folk rather than nomads.

Dr Bloch takes a keen interest in the irrigation systems of the time. I imagine if Saba had the engineering skills to create water systems then it would have been a fertile land, good for agriculture. If people were farmers, used to having water, they were unlikely to be well prepared for a desert existence.

So here I am suddenly sparring with an academic. I have my own argument, my own views. I am picking up some characteristics from the Queen of Sheba.

There is a poem about her by a Scottish writer, Kathleen Jamie, which exudes intellectual confidence. I can recite snatches of it.

Yes, we'd like to
clap the camels,
to smell the spice,
admire her hairy legs and
a bonny wicked smile, we want to take
PhDs in Persian, be vice
to her president: we want
to help her
ask some Difficult Questions
she's shouting for our wisest man
to test her mettle:
Scour Scotland for a Solomon!
Sure enough: from the back of the crowd
Someone growls:
Whae do you think y'ur?
And a thousand laughing girls and she
draw our hot breath
and shout:
The Queen of Sheba!

The Queen of Sheba yielded to Solomon's glory and wisdom and to his God. But she tested him hard first. There was no instant acceptance. It came at the end of a long intellectual journey.

This was a woman indeed who used her own alphabet.

Trade required communication. Merchants used seals, inventories were opened to check goods were in order. An intellectual class developed a pictographic script that became the alphabet. It was written on wood, stone and bronze. Dr Bloch has his eye on cuneiform inscriptions on a South Arabian abecedary on the edge of a stele from Marib dated the first century AD.

Dr Bloch's prize evidence for the kingdom of Saba comes from an inscription of Yitha'amar Watar found at Sirwah, in Yemen. Yitha'amar Watar, the rule of Saba, is mentioned in the inscriptions of Sargon II, King of Assyria from 721 to 705 BC. Generations of rulers before him are also mentioned in Sabaic inscriptions. Dr Bloch guesses that the Kingdom of Saba was founded in the eighth century BC. The early rulers of Saba had the title mkrb (mukarrib) meaning perhaps 'the unifier'. Could this mean a unified kingdom, as happened later in the Axumite kingdom? Just as Solomon wished to unify Israel and Judah, did the Queen of Sheba wish to unify the lands on either side of the Red Sea—Ethiopia and Yemen?

The exhibition broadens to address the kingdom of Himyar, on the southern tip of Yemen and the origins of the Yemenite Jews. The kingdom of Sheba was effectively annexed to Himyar in the third century AD. Dr Bloch is studying photographs of Zafar, the capital of southern Arabia until the Axumite conquest and mentioned in Aramaic inscription "… the city of Zafar in the land of the Himyarites…"

The exhibition seems to contain only one reference to Ethiopia's claims on the Queen of Sheba—a traditional Ethiopian painting, from 1971, depicting the story of Solomon and Sheba. I am getting used to the Queen of Sheba being cast in different nationalities and religions—and I'm interested to hear the notion of trade playing so explicitly.

Now I am finally to meet the great Solomon scholar, Israel Finkelstein at Tel Aviv University. He is a kind of Hebrew version of George Clooney, with pepper grey hair and an amused expression. He and his dear friend, the French biblical scholar Thomas Romer, are about to start a new adventure, excavating at a town outside Jerusalem called Abu Ghosh, or historically, the biblical site Kiryat Yearim.

I pass by it on the way, a peaceful French nunnery up on a hill, with meadow flowers and olive trees and in view fields of almond trees starting to blossom in spring, overseen by an enormous white statue of the Virgin Mary. Underneath a gnarled olive tree, a cheerful passage from Song of Solomon is written in stone. "The winter is past, the rain is over and gone, the flowers appear on the earth, the time for singing has come."

This is the site that Israel Finkelstein has identified, through the use of drones and the stimulated luminescence techniques, as the place that the Ark of the Covenant was kept before King David brought it to Jerusalem. According to Samuel, the Israelites brought the Ark into battle, suffered terrible losses and the Philistines captured the Ark. They fared no better. They were struck down with haemorrhoids and hastily sent the Ark back.

"And the men of Kiriath-Yearim came, and fetched the ark of the Lord and brought it into the house of Abinadab in the hill, and sanctified Eleazar his son to keep the ark of the Lord" (Samuel 7:1).

He and Thomas Romer are preparing to excavate. The time of singing has come. These distinguished but boyish figures are lauded in Israel, for biblical archaeologists are heroes because they lay claim to national destiny. Finkelstein himself has never over-egged biblical history. After all, he has described the sight of Jerusalem during the tenth century BC as a 'backwater'.

But he is convinced by the history of King David, because there is an independent Assyrian inscription for him outside the Bible and the figure of the soldier/ mercenary on the desert fringe before Judah developed as a kingdom, is historically plausible.

Solomon, he says, stretching out his legs and thinking aloud, is more difficult. He lacks the same written cross-references, but Professor Finkelstein is cautious about drawing conclusions. The independent attested evidence may be missing because it does not exist, or because we have not found it yet.

Little is known about the founders who pre-date the kings of Judah. Professor Finkelstein surmises that Solomon could be a territorial construct—an imagining of the golden past, to burnish and compete with the Northern Kingdom once the United Kingdom had become divided into Israel in the north and Judah in the south. That could explain the pride, for instance, in Solomon's horses, brought from the south to supply Assyrian chariots in the north.

Finkelstein has excavated Megiddo—or as it was later called, Armageddon—a 13-acre site dating from the tenth century BC in northern Israel with a labyrinth of stables that suggest there was a flourishing international horse trade. Assyrian texts record Israelite charioteers. Horses were highly regarded in Israel, the most admired being Kushite horses from the south of Egypt. According to the Bible, Solomon's horses were imported from Egypt and sold on to northern kingdoms, including the Hittites (whose territories later became part of Turkey) and the kings of Syria.

I have learned that there are three phrases of Solomon. Like the Queen of Sheba, he has multiple identities.

First is the story of his succession from David.

The second is the phase of magnificence, embellished by the presence of the Queen of Sheba. Here is the glory and the wisdom.

The third phase is Solomon the sinner, the hubristic king who looked abroad.

Israel wants to move the traditional dates for the Queen of Sheba, just as my radical archaeologists wanted to do in order to prove their Egyptian theory. Israel says that she fits naturally not into the tenth century BC, but into the seventh century, during which time Judah—the southern kingdom—is serving the demands of Assyrian trade, in Israel to the north. The king she would have visited, in his view, was not Solomon but Manasseh, son of Hezekiah, and a vassal of Assyria.

The evidence, he believes, is that Manasseh is rebuked in the Bible for his open trading policy. He is the king of globalisation. "Manasseh was in the globalisation camp and the camp that followed was more concerned about identity, about borders and boundaries. Solomon is a bit of a Manasseh."

Another sin of Manasseh was his religious tolerance. He allowed polytheism. Just as Solomon dallied with foreign deities, especially those of this Egyptian wife. The name YHWH appears in the ninth century BC, and the crackdown on female deities, such as Asherah begins. Thus the foundation of the Solomon and Sheba story, according to Professor Finkelstein, is the trade between southern Arabia, encouraged by the neo-Assyrians, via Judah.

"I think the Q of S is told as a background of historical reality—trade. This is as far as we can go. Romantic is good for Hollywood and in Ethiopia but we must see her in the background of the global economy of the time."

"What did President Clinton say?" smiles Professor Finkelstein. "It was 'the economy, stupid'. The Queen of Sheba represented globalisation."

With one comment, the professor strips away 3,000 years. His Queen of Sheba is suddenly an entirely modern character: trade is the great preoccupation of our age.

So here we are Britain and America wrestling with globalisation, power blocs and identity. And the flashpoint for superpower politics is the Gulf. It is the story of Solomon and the Queen of Sheba. Trade can be the route to peace. President Trump's peace plan in the Middle East has been controversial but one idea that captured the imagination was to free Gaza from its sea blockade in Israeli claimed waters by creating a new port. Cyprus could become the gateway to Gaza, policed by Israel.

Gaza was one of the great ports of the spice trade—it would be hopeful if it could trade by sea again. For now, the coast is a bleak area, awash with sewage, rather than a spice route.

The Queen of Sheba has other lessons of statesmanship for us. She ruled a country that was not conquered, although it apparently shared power between Ethiopia and Southern Arabia.

She husbanded water, recognising 3,000 years ago what we know now, which is that water is a finite source and its distribution is politically charged. Water also has religious properties.

Furthermore, she was both a rationalist and spiritual. Hearing of land and ruler of boastful glory she was determined to go to judge for herself. She asked hard questions. In an era of polemical news and propaganda information, it is imperative to judge for yourself.

The Queen of Sheba has an epic quality, linked as she is to Eve and to Mary and to the Day of Judgement. She spans faith and mythology and art and as Eyob Derillo first said: "Don't forget about Beyonce!"

As women struggle to establish their place in the new social order they could do with some role models. The Queen of Sheba is good enough for Beyonce and certainly good enough for me. She plays the long game.

She is a canvas on which we have all imposed our ideas of beauty, womanhood, virtue, power. And in a modern way, we have also demonised what we do not understand. If the Queen of Sheba frightened men through hairy legs, imagine what other forms of diversity can create alarm. Her period was exceptional for its profusion of female rulers. This turned out to be an aberration. But what if those times returned?

The Queen of Sheba feels too realised as a figure to be a mere symbol. Even her cameo role in the Bible and the Koran give her a strong sense of character. The oral tradition brings her vividly to life—a woman of sense and passion, human but related to the spirits, a diplomat, a trader, a lover. In art, she is both merry and transcendent. Women admire her, everyone desires her. She stands for light but also darkness. In Jewish legend, she becomes a night demon, and by the Middle Ages, she was also Lilith. So she is both associated with the fertility goddess Asherah, and with Lilith.

She is a temptress to Flaubert and in German Jewish folklore. Compare this to the Ethiopian worship of the Queen of Sheba. She is always portrayed in full face rather than profile, to denote purity. She is a virgin queen, tricked by Solomon into sexual relations. She is not hairy, and she has no genie heritage. There is no hoopoe bird but a wise adviser, Tamrin, on whom our stateswoman queen relies.

The Ethiopian version of the Queen of Sheba is perhaps the most faithful. At the end of my travels, I take my early chapters to show Eyob Derillo. We drink coffee in the sharp sunshine outside the British Library, by Kings Cross, London. He shows me a drawing that he has just found at the British Library of the Queen of Sheba arriving by horseback to see Solomon. It proves to him the significance of horses in the story. He says that this unseen picture and he is so pleased to contribute another step in our quest.

I confide to him that I have become more doubtful about the historical authenticity of the Queen of Sheba the more that I have consulted the experts. We really have no evidence.

Eyob says passionately: "I believe that she existed." He adds: "Don't you think she is treated as less credible because she is a woman? Look at her legacy! That has to be based on something."

She reminds me of the Ethiopian Church when challenged on the existence of the Ark of the Covenant at Axum. "Believe it or not, we know it is here." The point about the Ark is that it is hidden. Solomon and Sheba are cited as the wisdom of the occult.

As Israel Finkelstein said of Solomon, just because we have not found all the evidence yet, does not mean that Solomon and Sheba did not exist. There speaks an archaeologist, but it could also be a definition of faith.

The Queen of Sheba is vibrant but also hard to catch. I wonder if it is that her destiny eclipses even her. I return one last time to look at Claude Lorrain's painting of the Queen of Sheba at the National Gallery. The reason that Ana Maria Pacheco had been inspired by this painting to recreate the Queen of Sheba was that the figure in the painting was so tiny. Was it an artistic error to make the subject of the painting so hard to spot?

Instead, your eye is drawn to the path of light across the water, the ships heading out. The central message of the painting is not the woman descending the steps to the harbour, but the horizon.

Finally, I am left with my conversation with the Dean of Canterbury Cathedral, Robert Willis.

The significance of the Queen of Sheba, he had said was her voyage in the sea of creation. The message was the journey. She came to ask hard questions and was satisfied with the answers. That is a pretty sound metaphor for me. The reason the Queen of Sheba talks to us now is more than her race and beauty and feminism. It is that she embodies the journey. So long as we wish to pursue truth and discover meaning, we travel in her wake.

The sea quest is for knowledge. St Bartholomew sends an Ark of a cedar chest containing a palm twig, a Bible and a letter to the Arcadian land imagined by the Middle Ages. Paradise must be searched for.

My geographical journey has ended, but my search for wisdom continues. I no longer need to travel to find it.

The Queen of Sheba went on a long journey, for love, for trade and mostly for curiosity. She is a mystery, and that is the riddle of life. It is an unfolding mystery.

But her legacy was her son. The symbol of faith and wisdom, the Ark of the Covenant, the word of God, was brought home by Menelik. I liked this Ethiopia version of the Queen of Sheba's story the best. My heart is at home. When I return to Norfolk, my son tells me that he and his wife are expecting a baby. I am about to become a grandmother. If I could put my brimming happiness to music, it would be the joy and expectancy of Handel.

Resources

- *The Sign and the Seal: Quest for the Lost Ark of the Covenant*, Graham Hancock
- *David and Solomon: In Search of the Bible's Sacred Kings and the Roots of the Western Tradition: In Search of the Bible's Sacred Kings and the Roots*, Israel Finkelstein
- *The Orthodox Church of Ethiopia: A History*, John Binns
- *Queen of Sheba*, St John Philby
- *The Queen of Sheba's Land: Yemen*, Adnan Tarcici
- *The Invention of God*, Thomas Romer
- *Solomon and Sheba*, James B. Pritchard
- *The House of Islam: A Global History*, Ed Husain
- *Ethiopian Magic Scrolls*, Jacques Mercier
- *The Pale Abyssinian: The Life of James Bruce, African Explorer and Adventurer*, Miles Bredin
- *The Quest for the Ark of the Covenant: The True History of the Tablets of Moses*, Stuart Munro-Hay
- *Travel to Discover the Source of the Nile*, James Bruce
- *Holy Bible: King James Version (KJV)*, Collins Staff
- *Waugh in Abyssinia (Penguin Modern Classics)*, Evelyn Waugh
- *Walking the Bible: A Journey by Land Through the Five Books of Moses*, Bruce Feiler
- *Sabaean Inscriptions from Mahram Bilquis*, John Randall
- *The Prince of the Marshes: And Other Occupational Hazards of a Year in Iraq*, Rory Stewart
- *An Introduction to the Archaeology of Ancient Egypt*, Bard Kathryn
- *Who We Are and How We Got Here: Ancient DNA and the New Science of the Human Past*, David Reich

- *Song of Songs (2005): Commentary (The Old Testament Library)*, J. Cheryl Exum
- *The Song of Songs and the Ancient Egyptian Love Songs*, Michael V. Fox
- *VISIO Pacis, Holy City and Grail: An Attempt at an Inner History of the Grail Legend*, Adolf Helen
- *W.B. Yeats and the Muses*, Joseph M. Hassett
- *Integrity of Yeats (T. Davis Lecture)*, Denis Donoghue
- *Piero Della Francesca*, Longhi, Roberto
- *On Beauty: A History of a Western Idea*, Umberto Eco
- *Thus Spoke Zarathustra*, Friedrich Nietzsche
- *Saladin: Hero of Islam*, Geoffrey Hindley
- *Sources of the Grail*, John Matthews
- *The Crusades Through Arab Eyes (Saqi Essentials)*, Amin Maalouf
- *The Queen of Sheba*, Jamie Kathleen
- *Ancient Yemen + Milton: A Poem, Blake, William + The Worship of the Serpent*, John Bathurst Deane
- *A Time to Keep Silence*, Patrick Leigh Fermor
- *From the Exodus to King Akhnaton*, Immanuel Velikovsky
- *Hiram King of Tyre, Grand Master of the Long Ages Gone*, Frank C. Higgins
- Hasmonean Realities behind Ezra, Nehemiah, and Chronicles, Israel Finkelstein
- *Francis: A Life in Songs*, Ann Wroe
- *Pythagoras*, Thomas Stanley
- *From the Beast to The Blonde: On Fairy Tales and Their Tellers*, Marina Warner
- *Stranger Magic: Charmed States & the Arabian Nights*, Marina Warner
- *Enigmas and Riddles in Literature*, Eleanor Cook
- *Ecstasies: Deciphering the Witches' Sabbath*, Carlo Ginzburg
- *The Kebra Nagast: A Book of Rastafarian Wisdom*, Gerald Hausman
- *Rabbinic Fantasies, Imaginative Narratives from Classical Hebrew Literature (Yale Judaica Series)*, David Stern
- *Hatshepsut: From Queen to Pharaoh*, Catharine H. Roehrig
- *Grimoires: A History of Magic Books*, Owen Davies
- *Foucault's Pendulum*, Umberto Eco

- *Aspects of the Maritime Silk Road: from the Persian Gulf to the East China Sea 9 East Asian Economic and Socio-Cultural Studies)*, Ralph Kauz
- *Qataban and Sheba: Exploring ancient kingdoms on the Biblical spice route of Arabia*, Wendell Phillips
- *Religion and Medicine in the Middle Ages (3) (York Studies in Medieval Theology*, Peter Biller
- *River in the Desert: A History of the Negev*, Nelson Glueck
- *Spice: The History of a Temptation*, Jack Turner
- *The Horsemen of Israel: horses and Chariotry in Monarchic Israel (History, Archaeology and Culture of the Levant*, Deborah T. Combs Cantrell
- *Lords of the Desert: Britain's Struggle with America to Dominate the Middle East*, Barr James
- *The Qur'an (Oxford World's Classics)*, M. A. S. Abdel Haleem
- *The History of the Suez Canal: A Personal Narrative (Classic Reprint)*, Monsieur Ferdinand de Lesseps
- *British Military Operations in Aden and Radfan: 100 Years of British Colonial Rule*, Nick van der Bijl
- *Sheba: Through the Desert in Search of the Legendary Queen*, Nicholas Clapp

9 781398 460669